S0-BKP-051

The New Workplace

Other Titles by Pegasus Communications, Inc.

Anthologies
Managing the Rapids: Stories from the Forefront of the Learning Organization
Reflections on Creating Learning Organizations

The Pegasus Workbook Series
Systems Archetype Basics: From Story to Structure
Systems Thinking Basics: From Concepts to Causal Loops

The "Billibonk" Series
Billibonk & the Thorn Patch
Frankl's "Thorn Patch" Fieldbook
Billibonk & the Big Itch

Human Dynamics
Human Dynamics: A New Framework for Understanding People and Realizing the
    Potential in Our Organizations

The Innovations in Management Series
From Mechanistic to Social Systemic Thinking: A Digest of a Talk
    by Russell L. Ackoff
Applying Systems Archetypes
Toward Learning Organizations: Integrating Total Quality Control
    and Systems Thinking
Designing a Systems Thinking Intervention: A Strategy for Leveraging Change
The Natural Step: A Framework for Achieving Sustainability in Our Organizations
Anxiety in the Workplace: Using Systems Thinking to Deepen Understanding
The Soul of Corporate Leadership: Guidelines for Values-Centered Governance
Creating Sustainable Organizations: Meeting the Economic, Ecological, and Social
    Challenges of the 21st Century
Creating Value: Linking the Interests of Customers, Employees, and Investors

The Toolbox Reprint Series
Systems Archetypes I: Diagnosing Systemic Issues and Designing
    High-Leverage Interventions
Systems Archetypes II: Using Systems Archetypes to Take Effective Action
Systems Thinking Tools: A User's Reference Guide

Newsletters
The Systems Thinker™
Leverage: News and Ideas for the Organizational Learner™

The New Workplace

Transforming
the Character
and Culture
of Our Organizations

Compiled from
The Systems Thinker™ *Newsletter*

PEGASUS COMMUNICATIONS, INC.

WALTHAM

CHABOT COLLEGE LIBRARY

HD
58.8
.N492
1998

**The New Workplace: Transforming the Character
and Culture of Our Organizations**
Copyright ©1998 by Pegasus Communications, Inc.
First Printing: May 1998

All rights reserved. No part of this book may be reproduced or transmitted in any
form or by any means, electronic or mechanical, including photocopying and
recording, or by any information storage or retrieval system, without written permission from the publisher.

Library of Congress Cataloging-in-Publication Data

The new workplace : transforming the character and culture of our organizations /
compiled from *The Systems Thinker*™ Newsletter.

p. cm.
ISBN 1-883823-25-0
1. Organizational change. 2. Leadership. I. *The Systems Thinker*

HD58.8.N492   1998
658.4' 06--dc21

98-14807
CIP

Acquiring editor: Kellie Wardman O'Reilly
Project editor: Lauren Johnson
Design and production: Thompson Steele Production Services
Cover design: Fineline

Pegasus Communications, Inc. is dedicated to providing resources that help people
explore, understand, articulate, and address the challenges they face in managing the
complexities of a changing world. Since 1989, Pegasus has worked to build a community of organizational learning practitioners through **The Systems Thinker**™
and **Leverage** newsletters, books, audio and video tapes, and its annual **Systems
Thinking in Action**™ **Conference** and other events. For more information, contact:

Pegasus Communications, Inc.
One Moody Street
Waltham, MA 02154–5339
Phone: (781) 398-9700   Fax: (781) 894-7175
PEGASUS   www.pegasuscom.com
COMMUNICATIONS

♻ Printed on recycled paper.

5000

Acknowledgments

Thank you to all the individuals who are using the principles, tools, and disciplines of organizational learning to help transform today's workplace. In particular, thanks to the contributing authors of *The New Workplace* for their efforts to develop new ways of working together, and for sharing their thoughts. This book would not exist without their passion, clarity, and innovative spirit.

The essays in this book first appeared in *The Systems Thinker* Newsletter and were edited by Colleen Lannon, Daniel H. Kim, Kellie Wardman O'Reilly, Janice Molloy, and Lauren Johnson.

Contents

From Fragmentation to Integration: Building Learning
Communities
by Peter M. Senge and Daniel H. Kim   1

P a r t   O n e   *Rethinking the Purpose of Work*

1   Is There More to Corporations Than Maximizing Profits?
by Bryan Smith and Art Kleiner   13

2   The "Living" Company: Extending the Corporate Lifeline
by Arie de Geus   21

P a r t   T w o   *Creating New Concepts in Leadership*

3   Transforming the Character of a Corporation
by Bill O'Brien   33

4   Rethinking Leadership in the Learning Organization
by Peter M. Senge   43

P a r t   T h r e e   *Envisioning and Building Learning Communities*

5   Can Learning Cultures Evolve?
     by Edgar H. Schein   59

6   The Inner Game of Work: Building Capability
     in the Workplace
     by Tim Gallwey   69

7   Creating a New Workplace: Making a Commitment to
     Community
     by Greg Zlevor   81

8   Building a Core Competence in Community
     by Kazimierz Gozdz   91

9   The Learning Organization Journey: Assessing
     and Valuing Progress
     by Nils Bohlin and Paul Brenne   103

     About the Authors   113
     Additional Resources   117
     Index to *The Systems Thinker*   119

From Fragmentation to Integration: Building Learning Communities

by Peter M. Senge and Daniel H. Kim

"We live in an era of massive institutional failure," says Dee Hock, founder and CEO emeritus of Visa International. We need only look around us to see evidence to support Dee's statement. Corporations, for example, are spending millions of dollars to teach high-school graduates in their workforces to read, write, and perform basic arithmetic. Our healthcare system is in a state of acute crisis. The U.S. spends more on healthcare than any other industrialized country, and yet the health of our citizens is the worst among those same nations. Our educational system is increasingly coming under fire for not preparing our children adequately to meet the demands of the future. Our universities are losing credibility. Our religious institutions are struggling to maintain relevance in people's lives. Our government is increasingly dysfunctional, caught in a vicious cycle of growing special interest groups, distrust, and corruption. The corporation may be the healthiest institution in the U.S. today, which isn't saying much.

One of the reasons for this widespread institutional failure is that the *knowledge-creating system*, the method by which human beings collectively learn and by which society's institutions improve and revitalize themselves, is deeply fragmented. This fragmentation has developed so gradually that few of us have noticed it; we take the disconnections between the branches of knowledge and between knowledge and practice as a given.

A Knowledge-Creating System

Before we can address the issue of fragmentation, we need to establish what has been fragmented. In other words, what do we mean by a knowledge-creating system, and what does it mean to say it is fragmented?

We believe that human communities have always attempted to organize themselves to maximize the production, transmittal, and application of knowledge. In these activities, different individuals fulfill different roles, with varying degrees of success. For example, in indigenous cultures, elders articulate timeless principles grounded in their experience to guide their tribes' future actions. "Doers," whether warriors, growers, hunters, or nannies, try to learn how to do things better than before and continually improve their craft. And coaches and teachers help people develop their capacities to both perform their roles and grow as human beings. These three activities—which we can term theory-building, practice, and capacity-building—are intertwined and woven into the fabric of the community in a seamless process that restores and advances the knowledge of the tribe. One could argue that this interdependent knowledge-creating system is the only way that human beings collectively learn, generate new knowledge, and change their world.

We can view this system for producing knowledge as a cycle. People apply available knowledge to accomplish their goals. This practical application in turn provides experiential data from which new theories can be formulated to guide future action. New theories and principles then lead to new methods and tools that translate theory into practical know-how, the pursuit of new goals, and new experience—and the cycle continues.

Imagine that this cycle of knowledge-creation is a tree (see "The Cycle of Knowledge-Creation"). The tree's roots are the theories. Like theories, the roots are invisible to most of the world, and yet the health of the root system to a large extent determines the health of the tree. The branches are

THE CYCLE OF KNOWLEDGE-CREATION

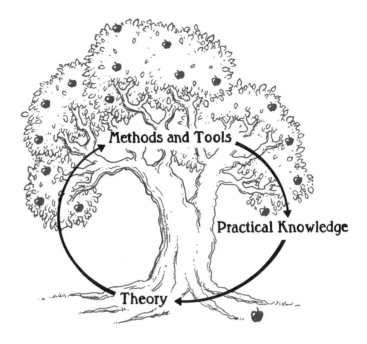

Like theories, the tree's roots are invisible, and yet the health of the root system determines the health of the tree. The branches are the methods and tools, which enable translation of theories into new capabilities and practical results. The fruit is that practical knowledge. The tree as a whole is a system.

the methods and tools, which enable translation of theories into new capabilities and practical results. The fruit is that practical knowledge. In a way, the whole system seems designed to produce the fruit. But, if you harvest and eat *all* the fruit from the tree, eventually there will be no more trees. So, some of the fruit must be used to provide the seeds for more trees. The tree as a whole is a system.

The tree is a wonderful metaphor, because it functions through a profound, amazing transformational process called photosynthesis. The roots absorb nutrients from the soil. Eventually, the nutrients flow through the trunk and into the branches and leaves. In the leaves, the nutrients interact with sunlight to create complex carbohydrates, which serve as the basis for development of the fruit.

So, what are the metaphorical equivalents that allow us to create fruits of practical knowledge in our organizations? We can view research activities as expanding the root system to build better and richer theories. Capacity-building activities extend the branches by translating the theories into usable methods and tools. The use of these methods and tools enhances people's capabilities. The art of practice in a particular line of work transforms the theories, methods, and tools into usable knowledge as people apply their capabilities to practical tasks, much as the process of photosynthesis converts the nutrients into leaves, flowers, and fruit. In our society,

- **Research** represents any disciplined approach to discovery and understanding with a commitment to share what's being learned. We're not referring to white-coated scientists performing laboratory experiments; we mean research in the same way that a child asks, "What's going on here?" By pursuing such questions, research—whether performed by academics or thoughtful managers or consultants reflecting on their experiences—continually generates new theories about how our world works.

- **Practice** is anything that a group of people does to produce a result. It's the application of energy, tools, and effort to achieve something practical. An example is a product development team that wants to build a better product more quickly at a lower cost. By directly applying the available theory, tools, and methods in our work, we generate practical knowledge.

- **Capacity-building** links research and practice. It is equally committed to discovery and understanding and to practical know-how and results. Every learning community includes coaches, mentors, and teachers—people who help others build skills and capabilities through developing new methods and tools that help make theories practical.

"The Stocks and Flows of Knowledge-Creation" shows how the various elements are linked together in a knowledge-creating system.

Institutionalized Fragmentation

If knowledge is best created by this type of integrated system, how did our current systems and institutions become so fragmented? To answer that question, we need to look at how research, practice, and capacity-building are institutionalized in our culture (see "The Fragmentation of Institutions," p. 6).

THE STOCKS AND FLOWS OF KNOWLEDGE-CREATION

Research activities build better and richer theories. Capacity-building functions translate the theories into usable methods and tools. The use of these methods and tools enhances people's capabilities. The art of practice transforms the theories, methods, and tools into practical knowledge, as people apply their capabilities to practical tasks.

For example, what institution do we most associate with research? Universities. What does the world of practice encompass? Corporations, schools, hospitals, and nonprofits. And what institution do we most associate with capacity-building—people helping people in the practical world? Consulting, or the HR function within an organization. Each of these institutions has made that particular activity its defining core. And, because research, practice, and capacity-building each operate within the walls of separate institutions, it is easy for the people within these institutions to feel cut off from each other, leading to suspicion, stereotyping, and an "us" versus "them" mindset.

Technical Rationality: One Root of Fragmentation

How did we reach this state of fragmentation? Over hundreds of years, we have developed a notion that knowledge is the province of the expert, the researcher, the academic. Often, the very term *science* is used to connote

THE FRAGMENTATION OF INSTITUTIONS

Because research, practice, and capacity-building each operate within the walls of separate institutions, the people within these institutions feel cut off from each other, leading to suspicion, stereotyping, and an "us" versus "them" mindset.

this kind of knowledge, as if the words that come out of the mouths of scientists are somehow inherently more truthful than everyone else's words.

Donald Schön has called this concept of knowledge "technical rationality." First you develop the theory, then you apply it. Or, first the experts come in and figure out what's wrong, and then you use their advice to fix the problem. Of course, although the advice may be brilliant, sometimes we just can't figure out how to implement it.

But maybe the problem isn't in the advice. Maybe it's in the basic assumption that this method is how learning or knowledge-creation actually works. Maybe the problem is really in this very way of thinking: that first you must get "the answer," then you must apply it.

The implicit notion of technical rationality often leads to conflict between executives and the front-line people in organizations. Executives often operate by the notion of technical rationality: In Western culture, being a boss means having all the answers. However, front-line people know much more than they can ever say about their jobs and about the organization. They actually have the capability to *do* something, not just *talk* about something. Technical rationality is great if all you ever have to do is talk.

Organizing for Learning

If we let go of this notion of technical rationality, we can then start asking more valuable questions, such as:

- How does real learning occur?
- How do new capabilities develop?
- How do learning communities that interconnect theory and practice, concept and capability come into being?
- How do they sustain themselves and grow?
- What forces can destroy them, undermine them, or cause them to wither?

Clearly, we need a theory, method, and set of tools for organizing the learning efforts of groups of people.

Real learning is often far more complex—and more interesting—than the theory of technical rationality suggests. We often develop significant new capabilities with only an incomplete idea of *how we do what we do*. As in skiing or learning to ride a bicycle, we "do it" before we really understand the actual concept. Similarly, practical know-how often precedes new principles and general methods in organizational learning. Yet, this pattern of learning can also be problematic.

For example, teams within a large institution can produce significant innovations, but this new knowledge often fails to spread. Modest improvements may spread quickly, but real breakthroughs are difficult to diffuse. Brilliant innovations won't spread if there is no way for them to spread; in other words, if there is no way for an organization to extract the general lessons from such innovations and develop new methods and tools for sharing those lessons. The problem is that wide diffusion of learning requires the same commitment to research and capacity-building as it does to practical results. Yet few businesses foster such commitment. Put differently, organizational learning requires a *community* that enhances research, capacity-building, and practice.

Learning Communities

We believe that the absence of effective learning communities limits our ability to learn from each other, from what goes on within the organization, and from our most clearly demonstrated breakthroughs. Imagine a learning community as a group of people that bridges the worlds of research, practice, and capacity-building to produce the kind of knowledge that has the power to transform the way we operate, not merely make incremental improvements. If we are interested in innovation and in the vitality of large institutions, then we are interested in creating learning communities that *integrate* knowledge instead of fragment it.

In a learning community, people view each of the three functions—research, capacity-building, practice—as vital to the whole (see "A Learning Community"). Practice is crucial because it produces tangible results that show that the community has learned something. Capacity-building is important because it makes improvement possible. Research is also key because it provides a way to share learning with people in other parts of the organization and with future generations within the organization. In a learning community, people assume responsibility for the knowledge-creating process.

Learning Communities in Action

To commit to this knowledge-creating process, we must first understand what a learning community looks like in action in our organizations. Imagine a typical change initiative in an organization; for example, a product development team trying a new approach to the way they handle engineering changes. Traditionally, such a team would be primarily interested in improving the results on their own projects. Team members probably wouldn't pay as much attention to deepening their understanding of why a new approach works better, or to creating new methods and tools for others to use. Nor would they necessarily attempt to share their learnings as widely as possible—they might well see disseminating the information as someone else's responsibility.

In a learning community, however, from the outset, the team conceives of the initiative as a way to maximize learning for itself *as well as* for other teams in the organization. Those involved in the research process are integral members of the team, not outsiders who poke at the system from a disconnected and fragmented perspective. The knowledge-creating process functions in real time within the organization, in a seamless cycle of practice, research, and capacity-building.

A LEARNING COMMUNITY

Capacity-Building

Research   **Practice**

In a learning community, people view each of the three functions—research, capacity-building, practice—as vital to the whole.[1]

[1] The origins of this diagram unfolded as follows: The MIT Organizational Learning Center (OLC) Design Team first depicted the research, practice, and capacity-building activities as three interlocked circles in its thinking about learning communities. The diagram took its final form when John Shibley drew it as three interweaving "spheres of influence" during a meeting of the "Animators Group" at the OLC. The Three Spiral Diagram has since become a central metaphor for learning communities.

Imagine if this were the way in which we approached learning and change in all of our major institutions. What impact might this approach have on the health of any of our institutions, and on society as a whole? Given the problems we face within our organizations and within the larger culture, do we *have* any choice but to seek new ways to work together to face the challenges of the future? We believe the time has come for us to begin the journey back from fragmentation to wholeness and integration. The time has come for true learning communities to emerge. ⤝

Peter M. Senge is a senior lecturer at the Massachusetts Institute of Technology, where he is part of the Organizational Learning and Change group. He is also chairman of the Society for Organizational Learning (SoL). He is the author of the widely acclaimed book *The Fifth Discipline: The Art and Practice of the Learning Organization*, and, with colleagues Charlotte Roberts, Rick Ross, Bryan Smith, and Art Kleiner, coauthor of *The Fifth Discipline Fieldbook: Strategies and Tools for Building a Learning Organization*.

Daniel H. Kim, PhD, is publisher of *The Systems Thinker* and a trustee on the governing council of the Society for Organizational Learning. He is a well-regarded author as well as an international public speaker, facilitator, and teacher of systems thinking and organizational learning.

Part One

⬎

Rethinking
the
Purpose
of
Work

The task of creating learning communities in the world of work cannot be separated from questions about purpose, leadership, and implementation. Accordingly, Part One examines the role of purpose as the bedrock of organizational life. In "Is There More to Corporations than Maximizing Profits?" Bryan Smith and Art Kleiner boldly challenge a long-held, widespread belief about why businesses need exist. The authors invite us to resist the siren call of short-term profits as the primary goal of a business, and to instead reconnect with our organization's sense of core purpose. As they point out, this very reconnecting with purpose can itself lead to dramatic short-term results.

In "The 'Living' Company: Extending the Corporate Lifeline," Arie de Geus takes the discussion about purpose to the next level. De Geus shows how a company's view of its human community plays a primary role in how long it will survive. He contrasts the metaphors of company-as-machine and company-as-living-system, and invites us to explore the ramifications of each.

Chapter One

Is There More to Corporations than Maximizing Profits?

by Bryan Smith and Art Kleiner

"The sole purpose of a corporation is to maximize return on investment to shareholders." That is the *raison d'être* for most organizations—and many believe it is pointless to develop any other purpose. Proponents of this belief say that any loyal, dedicated officer of a company should have no aspirations aside from providing good financial results as quickly as possible. While the assumption is prevalent, it contradicts the very foundation of learning organization principles and beliefs. According to Peter Senge, it is "the most insidious idea that has crept into mainstream Western management in the last 30 to 40 years."

Obviously, making money is important. A manager who says profit is unimportant is like a coach who says, "I don't care if we win or lose." Both lose credibility in their ability to bring out the best in their teams. But to confuse an essential requirement for success with an organization's actual purpose is like thinking that breathing is the primary reason for living. Our entire industrial enterprise has been crippled by this erroneous assumption. Yet it is so deeply ingrained that in many circles, anyone who questions it may immediately be called crazy themselves (see "The Roots of the Notion," on page 18–19).

SIR, THE COMMITTEE HAS DONE IT! WE'VE GOT THE VISION, MISSION AND PURPOSE DOWN TO TWO WORDS: BOTTOM LINE!

"Shifting the Burden" to Return on Investment

Regardless of the origin of the mental model that profitability equals core purpose, managers still feel hamstrung by it. Many feel they can't focus on core purpose as long as they are bound by this frantic need for short-term profits. But it is a Catch-22: To ultimately meet medium- and long-term bottom-line demands, they must focus on core purpose.

These managers and their organizations are caught in a "Shifting the Burden" dynamic, where a more immediately appealing "quick fix" impairs a system's ability to address the real root causes of a problem (see "Dangers of Bottom-Line Thinking"). The fundamental solution to this bottom-line focus is a potentially lengthy, soul-searching effort to develop a sense of core purpose and build strong relationships with investors, customers, and employees (B2). Since this kind of process is slow and seemingly risky, many managers opt for the quicker fix: "We'll show investors we can enhance returns by doing something really dramatic *right now*." Declaring "the purpose of our company is maximizing return on investment to stockholders,"

DANGERS OF "BOTTOM-LINE THINKING

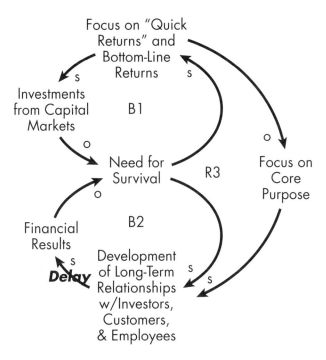

A company facing difficult times can enter a long process of developing better relationships with key stakeholders to improve its financial standing (B2), or focus on quick, bottom-line actions such as cutting staff to attract outside investment (B1). Focusing on quick results, however, can take attention away from a deeper look at the company's purpose, which could weaken stakeholder relationships and threaten the long-term survival of the company (R3).

they institute tough financial measures, hastily cutting staff and R&D. Improved financial statements attract investment from capital markets, which allows them to survive in the short term (B1).

But this strategy has dangerous side-effects. While this stance attracts short-term capital, it also demands even more short-term bottom-line measures. The managers' fear of becoming controlled by the numbers becomes a self-fulfilling prophecy. And to long-term investors, this approach telegraphs a lack of focus on the business itself.

Customers.   Meanwhile, the company has also sent an implicit message to customers: "The fundamental purpose of our firm is returning investment to shareholders. We merely depend upon you for our revenues." Which can be interpreted as: "We're willing to make money off you in any way we can." This may be one of the key causes of eroding brand loyalty, because customers realize (possibly through a decline in product quality or through more aggressive marketing) that the customer relationship is no longer fundamental. The eroding loyalty in turn reinforces the belief among managers that customers only care about price. Over time, the company can drift into becoming a low value-added commodity producer.

Employees.   In addition, the implicit message of a "return on investment" focus for employees is the same: "Our purpose is to use you as a resource and make a buck off your back in whatever way we can." This intangible factor often evokes bitter, expensive labor-management battles and sharp declines in morale. Any company that focuses all its energies toward maximizing profits has a remarkably different feel than one where personal and shared visions are as important as monthly financial statements.

Top Management.   A similar pressure bears on the top management team. The new short-term focus adds powerful reinforcement to the idea that managers should put aside their personal wants, aspirations, feelings, and desires to add value, and focus on the corporation's financial measures. The senior managers' potential vision, creative force, and effort thus remain untapped. The managers become like sports players who spend every possible moment looking over their shoulders at the score board instead of focusing on the game.

The Alternative: Building Purpose from Scratch

In "Shifting the Burden" structures, the greatest leverage always comes from finding your way back to the fundamental solution. This may mean weaning your company from the "maximum return" addiction and raising capital by aligning investors, employees, and customers with your purpose and vision.

At Hanover Insurance, for example, former president Bill O'Brien spent 20 years defining his company's vision, values, and sense of common purpose. "In those days," he explains, "when mainstream businessmen believed the only purpose of business was making money, we were very radical. We said that the purpose of our company was three-fold: to give the American people the maximum value for their property and liability insurance dollar, to provide each employee with the help and environment necessary to become all he or she was capable of becoming, and to earn a profit to fuel our growth, provide for a rainy day, and reward ourselves. It was a mission statement, although nobody had heard of that word yet."

Part of O'Brien's work at Hanover involved developing a set of core values by which the company and all of the employees would operate (see "Transforming the Character of a Corporation," p. 33). These included:

- *merit*—making decisions based on intended results, not on politics;
- *openness*—being more honest in communications among employees and with shareholders;
- *localness*—making decisions at the level closest to the problem.

These principles helped operationalize the vision in a way that all stakeholders could see and understand. For example, the value of openness led to a rethinking of how shareholder reports were written. According to O'Brien, "I had worked in four companies before Hanover, and had seen first-hand how sometimes the reports to shareholders were not forthright interpretations of actual performance. . . . Not only did the shareholders tend to see through this, but it also made it impossible for employees to trust us. . . . At Hanover, starting in the 1970s, we sent the same report to front-line managers as we sent the board of directors, with no spin on the news."

The alternative to the hard work of clarifying vision and values that occurred at Hanover is to arm yourself against potential invaders and maintain a high stock price at all costs. But this cultivates a negative vision, and negative visions tend to backfire. Building a corporation whose stock price reflects the value we create, on the other hand, can be a positive, motivating experience for all employees.

THE ROOTS OF THE NOTION

Some people believe the "core purpose = ROI" mentality owes its popularity to strategic consultants, business school professors, and stock analysts. But like all cultural values, this assumption has deeper roots. Several (rarely challenged) tacit inferences lie behind it.

Corporations are "property."

Many people, even those with financial experience, buy into the assumption that "owning" a corporation is like "owning" a car—that a dominant shareholder has a free rein with their "property." The modern corporate form, however, is a direct descendant of the royal charters to joint-stock companies, in which monarchs granted sea captains immunity from debtor's liabilities in order to encourage them to take risks. While its form has varied, the corporation has essentially been the same ever since—a contract between shareholders, government, managers, and (with the development of labor law) employees.

Owning a share of a corporation is thus like owning a piece of a contract—you can buy and sell your share in it, and you may even be able to dominate it for a time, but you cannot single-handedly control the entire enterprise. Even the takeover artists of the 1980s discovered that the value of their purchases depended in part on the cooperation and commitment of people in the firm.

Corporations are sheep surrounded by wolves.

Another mental model states that corporate structures, *by their nature,* are vulnerable to leveraged buyouts and hostile takeovers unless they maintain a bottom-line focus. Writer Peter Drucker traces the roots of this assumption to the 1950s and 1960s, when senior managers were accountable only to "rubber-stamp" boards of directors. When the more turbulent 1970s and early 1980s came, these managers were unprepared for vulnerability. To keep share prices from dropping precipitately, some pursued desperate measures—including concealing their real financial performance.

Based on the memory of those frenetic, emotionally trying times, many managers and stock analysts have assumed that vulnerability is an innate part of corporate life. But it is only innate for some firms. Even at the height of the "greed era," companies with steady, long-term performance (like Johnson & Johnson) tended to have substantial market capitalization—and thus little to fear from takeovers.

(continued on next page)

THE ROOTS OF THE NOTION, *continued*

Stockholders want only the fastest, largest return on their investment.

Shareholders typically don't say why they are selling stock; it remains for analysts to explain a falling stock price by pointing to poor performance or lack of cost-cutting. But what do shareholders *really* want? Clearly, they want good returns, but it is naive to assume that they want profits at the expense of the company's long-term success.

Many investors primarily want to be participants in a viable, successful enterprise whose leadership they respect and trust, who they know won't lie to them, and who can competently sustain long-term performance. As Warren Buffett, the pre-eminent American investor, put it: "I look for a business where I think I know in a general way what is going to happen." That is why experienced investors always ask one question of entrepreneurs seeking capital: "In this venture, what are *you* putting at risk?"

Pension funds, which own 40% of all U.S. corporate stock, are particularly interested in long-term steady growth. Transaction costs are expensive for them, and one of their main objectives is avoiding risk—"For God's sake, don't lose our pensioners' money!" Increasingly, other investors also have non-financial agendas; the investors behind the "Ceres Principles," for instance, ask companies to agree to 10 basic principles of environmental practice. Some labor unions are also using their pension fund investments to lobby corporations to keep jobs in their home countries.

Managers spend (and often squander) shareholders' money.

This assumption implies that the money spent by corporations comes directly from shareholders. If they are not closely watched, senior managers will waste the money on political favors, ill-fated projects, and their own salaries and perks.

This belief may be true of some management, but is a great leap of abstraction to apply it to all. In reality, the shareholders are not "paying the bills." The revenues from sales are paying the bills. The shareholders are risking their money, within certain legal bounds, on the good faith and potential success of the enterprise. That good faith depends on the relationship between the CEO and investors, and on the company's credibility—both of which (in addition to the company's success) depend on its sense of long-term purpose.

Core Purpose and Performance

We have seen some powerful linkages between this work on defining core purpose and the deeper examination of a company's core competencies and economic value. Gary Hamel and C.K. Prahalad's work, for example, in *Competing for the Future*, describes the definition of a company's core competencies as key to developing an enduring competitive advantage for the future. It is not enough, they argue, to design new products and develop patents; a company must view the competencies that reside in those processes as their competitive advantage. However, identifying what areas to develop competence in requires a clear sense of organizational purpose.

Another approach that is complementary to clarifying core purpose and core competencies is EVA (Economic Value Added), an analytical framework that challenges many traditional notions of corporate financial performance, including narrow definitions of profitability and earnings per share. EVA is described in the book *The Quest for Value*, by G. Bennett Stewart III (Harper Collins, 1991), and has been used with substantial success by companies such as Coca-Cola and Quaker Oats.

Developing an enduring vision for an organization is not an immediate process, and it will certainly take longer than simply decreeing that all employees must produce more return to shareholders. Every organization's process for developing its sense of purpose will be different—depending in large part upon the current relationship between the company and its investors, employees, and customers. Building such a purpose means embarking on a developmental journey, but unless organizations begin the journey, they will, in effect, be adrift—with no purpose at all.

For more on developing a corporate strategy for building a shared vision, see "Building Shared Vision: How to Begin," *The Fifth Discipline Fieldbook* (New York: Doubleday, 1994), p. 312. Hanover Insurance's experience is described in more detail on p. 306 of the *Fieldbook*.

Bryan Smith is coauthor of *The Fifth Discipline Fieldbook* and president of Innovation Associates of Canada (Toronto, Ontario).

Art Kleiner is coauthor and editorial director of *The Fifth Discipline Fieldbook* (Doubleday, 1994) and author of *The Age of Heretics* (Doubleday, 1996), a history of the social movement to change large corporations for the better.

Chapter Two

The "Living" Company: Extending the Corporate Lifeline

by Arie P. de Geus

I n the 1970s, diversification was the rage. But by the early 1980s, serious doubts had surfaced in the Shell Group about the wisdom of moving the business portfolio away from oil and gas. Equal doubts persisted, however, about the long-term future of these resources. The company's leaders began to ask themselves, "Is there life after oil, or at some point will we be forced to return the company to the shareholders?"

To answer this question, Shell's planners set out to study other companies that had weathered significant changes and survived with their corporate identity intact. In particular, they were looking for companies that were older than Shell (100 years or more) and that were as important in their own industries. After some research, a few examples started trickling in: Du Pont, the Hudson Bay Company, W.R. Grace, Kodak, Mitsui, Sumitomo, Daimaru. Forty companies were eventually identified, of which 27 were studied in detail.

Keys to Longevity

Of the tens of thousands of companies that had existed at the beginning of the 19th century, why did so few remain by 1980? And what had these few done to survive? Shell's planners found that, in general, the 27 long-estab-

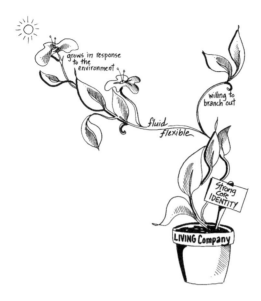

— Nancy Margulies

lished companies shared a history of adaptation to changing social, economic, and political conditions. The changes within those companies appeared to have occurred gradually, either in response to opportunity or in anticipation of customer demand. The companies shared some additional characteristics that could explain their durability:

• **Conservative Financing.** These companies had an old-fashioned appreciation of money. They did not make business decisions based on intricate financial deals using other people's money. Rather, they understood that money-in-hand gave them the flexibility to take advantage of opportunities as they arose.

• **Sensitivity to the Environment.** The leaders of these companies were outward looking, and the companies were connected to their external environment in ways that promoted intelligence and learning. As a result, they were sensitive to changes and developments in the world. They saw changes early, drew conclusions quickly, and took action swiftly.

• **A Sense of Cohesion and Company Identity.** In numerous cases, the Shell researchers found a deep concern and interest in the human element of the company—a quality that was somewhat surprising for the times. Employees and management seemed to have a good understanding of what the company stood for, and they personally identified with it. Quite often, this value system had been brought in by the founder, and was occasionally formalized in a kind of company constitution.

- *Tolerance.* The companies had made full use of what we would call in modern terms "decentralized structures and delegated authorities." They did not insist on relevance to the original business as a criterion for selecting new business possibilities, nor did they value central control over moves to diversify. In other words, they had high tolerance for "activities in the margin."

Businesses: Economic Entities or Organisms?

The Shell planners summed up their profile of these corporate survivors as follows: "They are financially conservative, with a staff that identifies with the company and a management which is tolerant and sensitive to the world in which they live."

This definition of a successful enterprise is quite different from the one I was taught in college, which portrayed businesses as rational, calculable, and controllable. Production, we learned, is a matter of costs and price. Costs are associated mostly with labor and capital—production factors that are interchangeable. If you have trouble with labor or if it is too expensive, you simply replace it with capital assets. For aspiring corporate leaders, this description of their future workplace painted a reassuring and comforting picture.

The real world, we discovered, was quite different. The economic theories offered at school made no mention of people, and yet the real workplace seemed to be full of them. And because the workplace teemed with people, it looked suspiciously as if companies were not always rational, calculable, and controllable.

The Shell study, which described within these companies a "struggle for survival, maintaining the institution in the face of a constantly changing world," supports this view that companies are perhaps more organic than economic in nature. Of course, the long-term survivors had to control costs, market their product, and update their technology, but they tended to see these basic functions as secondary to the more important considerations of life and death. These companies not only employed people who sometimes proved uncontrollable or irrational; the companies themselves behaved as if they were alive.

What if we were to look at companies as "living systems," rather than mere economic instruments created to produce goods and services? Would that viewpoint change our ideas about how to manage a business, or perhaps offer an explanation of why some companies endure and so many die young?

Though this hypothesis certainly does not apply to all companies—many do operate as if the production of goods and services is a purely economic problem—it may offer new insights into some corporate phenomena. In particular, I'd like to explore how "living" versus "economic" companies— and the management of them—differ in three basic respects:

- the role of profits and assets;
- the amount of steering and control from the top (in decisions such as diversification, downsizing, or expansion); and
- the way the company creates and shapes its human community.

Role of Profits and Assets

In the 27 companies Shell studied, the main driving force seemed to be the firm's own survival and the development of its potential. History shows that these companies engaged in a business—any business—so long as doing so sustained them as viable work communities. In fact, over their long lifetimes, each one changed its business portfolio at least once.

For example, Stora, a company that was not included in the original Shell study, began as a copper mine in central Sweden around the year 1288. During the next 700 years, new activities replaced the old "core" business: The company moved from copper to forest exploitation, to iron smelting, to hydro power, and, more recently, to paper and wood pulp and then chemicals.

Du Pont de Nemours started out as a gunpowder manufacturer, became the largest shareholder of General Motors in the 1930s, and now focuses mostly on specialty chemicals. Mitsui's founder opened a drapery shop in Edo (Tokyo) in 1673, went into money-changing, and then converted the company into a bank after the Meiji Restoration in the 19th century. The company later added coal mining, and toward the end of the 19th century it ventured into manufacturing.

In retrospect, each one of these portfolio changes might seem Herculean. But for the people running these enterprises at the time, the shift may have been imperceptible at the outset. At some stage, these companies may have thought of themselves as bankers, while a later generation of their leaders viewed themselves as manufacturers. Such changes cannot come about if a company regards its assets as the essence of its existence.

This fluidity demonstrates an important attitude toward whatever "core" business the company happens to be doing at any moment. All businesses need to make a profit in order to stay alive, but neither the core business— nor the profits from it—must be the driving force. Businesses need profits in the same way that any living being needs oxygen: we need to *breathe* in order to live, but we do not live in order to breathe.

Businesses need profits in the same way that any living being needs oxygen: We need to breathe in order to live, but we do not live in order to breathe.

This attitude is quite different from the "economic" company, which engages in a particular business to make profits or to maximize shareholder value. For such a company, the core business is the essence of life, and profits are its purpose. This position can lead to the belief that the present asset base represents the essence of the company—that the company's purpose in life is to exploit this particular set of assets. In a crisis, such a business will scuttle people rather than assets to save its "balance sheet" (which quite appropriately records only physical assets).

The logical endpoint of this thinking would be: "We will liquidate the company and return the remaining value to the shareholder whenever the oil runs out." Such "corporate suicide" is uncommon among "living" companies, however. Because their main purpose is their survival and the development of their potential, they would sooner shift the asset base than allow the current assets to determine the death of the institution.

Steering and Control from the Top

The long-term survivors shared two ways of handling a shift in their core business: The new business was not required to be relevant to the original business, and the diversifications were not initiated from a central control point. This pattern suggests that the companies' managers were highly tolerant of "activities in the margin."

Tolerance levels—toward new people, ideas, or practices—differ from company to company. Both a low-tolerance and a high-tolerance approach have a place in business, but which strategy a company should pursue depends on the amount of control that company has over its environment.

A management policy of low tolerance can be very efficient, but it needs two conditions to be fulfilled: the company should have some control over the world in which it is operating, and this world should be relatively stable. In such a world, a company can aim for maximum results with minimum resources. To achieve its goal of minimum resources, however, management will have to exercise not only some control over its surrounding world, but also a high degree of control over all internal operations. In these companies, little room exists for delegated authority and freedom of action.

A company may be lucky enough to live in a world that happens to be stable. However, any business that endures for more than a few score years will inevitably face changes in the external world. In a shifting and uncontrollable world, any company with the desire to survive over the long term would be ill advised to rely on a management policy of high internal and external controls. The Shell study showed that the survivors did, in fact, follow a high-tolerance strategy by creating the internal space and freedom to cope with external changes.

High tolerance is inefficient and wasteful of resources, but it enables a company to adapt to a changing environment over which the company has no control. Moreover, high tolerance provides a means for gradually renewing the business portfolio without having to resort to diversification by top-down "diktat."

The spring ritual of pruning roses provides a good illustration of the different implications of a high-tolerance versus a low-tolerance strategy. If a gardener wants to have the largest and most glorious roses in the neighborhood, he or she will take a "low-tolerance" approach and prune hard—

reducing each rose plant to one to three stems, each of which is in turn limited to two or three buds. Because the plant is forced to put all its available resources into its "core business," it will likely produce some sizable, dazzling flowers by June.

However, if a severe night frost were to strike in late April or early May, the plant could well suffer serious damage to the limited number of shoots that remain. Worse, if the frost (or hungry deer, or a sudden invasion of green flies) is very serious, the gardener may not get any roses at all. In fact, he or she risks losing the main stems or even the entire plant.

Pruning hard is a dangerous policy in a volatile environment. If a gardener lives in an unpredictable climate, he or she may instead want to try a "high-tolerance" approach, leaving more stems on the plant and more buds per stem. This gardener may not grow the biggest roses in the neighborhood, but he or she will have increased the likelihood of producing roses not only this year, but also in future years.

This policy of high tolerance offers yet another benefit—in companies as well as gardens. "Pruning long" achieves a gradual renewal of the "portfolio." Leaving young, weaker shoots on the plant gives them the chance to grow and to strengthen, so that they can take over the task of the main shoots in a few years. Thus, a tolerant pruning policy achieves two ends: It makes it easier to cope with unexpected environmental changes, and it works toward a gradual restructuring of the plant.

Although this policy is not as efficient as hard pruning in its use of resources—since the marginal activities take resources away from the main stem—it is better suited to an unpredictable environment or one in which we have little control. And as the success of the long-term survivors indicates, diversifying by creating tolerance for activities in the margin has a better track record than diversification by dictum.

Creating and Shaping the Human Community

The way a company views its human community is the third area of distinction between economic companies and self-perpetuating organic companies. The fact that living companies want to survive far beyond the lifetime of any individual employee requires a different managerial attitude toward the shaping of its human community.

Economic companies are like puddles of rainwater—a collection of raindrops that have run together into a suitable hollow. From time to time, more drops are added, and from time to time (when the temperature heats up), the puddle starts to evaporate. But overall, puddles are relatively static. The drops stay in the same position most of the time, and some of the drops never seem to leave the puddle. In fact, the drops are the puddle.

"Living" companies, by contrast, are more like rivers. The river may swell or it may shrink, but it takes a long and severe drought for it to disappear altogether.

"Living" companies, by contrast, are more like rivers. The river may swell or it may shrink, but it takes a long and severe drought for it to disappear altogether. Unlike a puddle, the drops of water that form the river change at every moment in time, and its activity is far more turbulent. The river lasts many times longer than the drops of water that shaped it originally.

A company can become more like a river by introducing "continuity rules"—personnel policies that ensure a regular influx of new human talent. Continuity rules also stipulate a fixed moment of retirement for every member, without exception. These strict exit rules remind the incumbent management that they are only one link in a chain. Within this expanded perspective, leadership becomes more like stewardship. A leader takes over from someone else, and eventually hands the enterprise over to yet another person. In the meantime, the current leader tries to keep the shop as healthy as he or she received it, if not a bit healthier than before.

Companies that are seen as learning, living beings demand different thinking, not only about recruitment, but also about other aspects of human relations. This rethinking begins with a definition of self: Who are we? Who belongs to the institution, and whom shall we let in? Clarity on these points is essential for a living work community. Without it, there is no continuity.

Without continuity, there is no basis for mutual trust between the community and its individual members. And without trust, there is no cohesion and therefore no community.

This thinking varies dramatically from the human-relations practices required in an economic company, where the HR function is expected to fit people to the asset base of the company. People are seen as cogs to fit a wheel, "hands" to serve the machines, or "brains" to make the right type of calculation or do the most promising research. Recruitment numbers are determined by the need for capacity to satisfy the foreseen demand for the company's products. If the company has more demand than capacity to fulfill the demand, it adds new people and machines. When it has less demand, it reduces capacity by letting people go.

The type of people the company will admit or fire is defined mostly in terms of "skills": "We need 250 metal bashers," or "We have a surplus of paper pushers." Within this framework, "people" are not hired or fired, only "skills" are. The mutual obligation between company and individual is that of "delivering a skill against the payment of a remuneration," an agreement usually concluded under the umbrella of the country's social legislation or some collective labor agreement.

In the living institution, criteria for admitting or dismissing people more closely parallels those methods used in clubs, trade unions, or professional bodies. Good care is taken that the new members carry the right professional qualifications, but the company also strives for a kind of harmony between the individual and the company. The members and the institution share certain values and purposes, and they aim to harmonize their respective long-term goals.

In the "living" company, admission is not determined solely by capacity. Capacity issues are addressed via the outside world, not by increasing or decreasing the internal membership. A shortage of capacity therefore leads to more subcontracting. In Italy, for example, Benetton does only a minor part of its manufacturing with its own people. Benetton admits relatively few members to the inner core of its work community. In this case, the use of subcontractors has proven effective for acquiring capacity in a competitive industry with fluctuating demand.

The Choice

Many people in the business world may not want to create a living work community, and simply want to manage a corporate machine with the sole purpose of earning a living. However, the latter choice has important consequences.

People in economic companies enjoy fewer options in their managerial practices. In those companies, only a small group of people qualify to be "one of us," while the rest of the recruits become attachments to somebody else's money machine. The company culture will consequently reflect this relationship. Non-managers will be viewed—and will view themselves—as "outsiders" hired for their skills rather than members with full rights and obligations. Their loyalty to the company will never extend beyond performing the tasks necessary to earn a paycheck. The lack of common goals and low levels of trust will require a strengthening of hierarchical controls in order to make the money machine work effectively and efficiently. As a result, the ability to mobilize all of the company's human potential will be severely limited.

For such a company, a critical point comes when the succession of the inner community needs to be addressed. The absence of continuity rules or the reliance on the next generation of the family for corporate continuity will turn many of these money machines into "ships that pass in the night." In short, economic companies not only face difficulties trying to operate effectively within a changing environment, but they also have to overcome considerable obstacles in their internal management practices just to make it to the next generation. ⟜

This paper was originally presented at the Royal Society of Arts in London on January 25, 1995.

Arie de Geus was appointed executive vice president at the Royal Dutch/Shell Group in 1978 and was with the company for 38 years. He served as head of an advisory group to the World Bank from 1990 to 1993, and is a visiting fellow at London Business School. He is the author of the well-regarded *The Living Company* (Harvard Business School Press, 1997).

Creating
New
Concepts
in
Leadership

Thinking about the purpose of the new workplace leads to a related issue: that of the role of leadership. What does the typical leader of a learning community look like? How can leaders help redefine corporate life? Part Two contains compelling insights into these questions. In "Transforming the Character of a Corporation," Bill O'Brien emphasizes the importance of moral excellence for leaders, and presents four guiding principles for which every executive should strive. As O'Brien explains, it is the leader's duty not only to cultivate these values in his or her organization, but also to embody them and thus serve as an example for others.

In the second piece in this section—"Rethinking Leadership in the Learning Organization"—Peter Senge contrasts two vastly different models of leadership.

In one framework (the older, more traditional model), people look to top executives to effect change. Senge presents an alternative model of leaders as "those people who demonstrate their commitment through their actions," and who can be found in many places within an organization. He then explores how an intertwining of three kinds of leaders—local, executive, and internal network—creates a leadership vehicle far more powerful and versatile than the traditional hierarchical framework.

Chapter Three

Transforming the Character of a Corporation

by Bill O'Brien

"We judge others by what they do; we judge ourselves by our intentions."

"What you *do* thunders so loud, I can't hear what you *say*."

These two quotations capture the difficulties inherent in trying to change an organization from one that is considered "ordinary" by today's standards to one that strives to practice moral excellence. By "moral excellence," I mean more than just avoiding what is illegal, or simply conforming to contemporary ethical standards. Instead, I mean embracing age-old moral truths and pursuing their practice with the same vigor and commitment with which we strive toward technological, marketing, or financial success.

Why make such an investment in moral excellence? Because moral excellence drives human energy. Human energy—in the form of initiative, creativity, fortitude, and stamina—drives product and service excellence, which, in turn, enhances financial performance. In my estimation, the pursuit of moral excellence is the most effective and enduring way to energize organizations, because it taps into our noblest aspirations. In addition, it can engender a social ecology in our companies that fosters individual maturation and happiness.

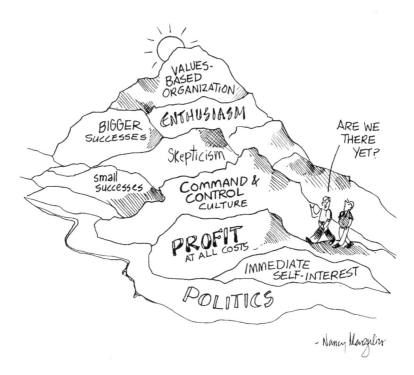

- Nancy Margulies

A Difficult Journey

Most employees want to be moral, and they prefer to spend their working lives in moral environments. Similarly, most leaders, including the members of the board of directors and CEO, want their organizations to be moral. Then why is it so difficult to transform an organizational culture to one based on moral excellence? I believe there are three reasons.

First, after decades of being treated as a herd of "hired hands," employees are highly skeptical of new schemes of governance. They say to themselves, "I hear what management says, but do they mean it? Will they personally practice what they preach?"

Second, most corporations have not undertaken major efforts to develop the philosophical and moral underpinnings of their governance systems. Most are based on a hodge-podge of notions derived, in part, from Roman army ideas about control, technological innovations aimed at maximizing efficiency, scientific principles about measurements, and lately some accommodations to Douglas McGregor's Theory Y. Few corporations have actually made a systematic effort to design their methods of governance in congruence with how human nature has evolved and is evolving.

Third, most managers have received minimal, if any, instruction about the moral dimension of exercising their responsibilities. Moral excellence in an organization must be undergirded by a network of managers who have paid attention to their own formation as human beings, a subject seldom found in the curriculum of our corporate management education programs or business schools.

Building a Culture to Foster Moral Excellence

So how does one begin the arduous task of retrofitting a corporation's culture to introduce the pursuit of moral excellence at its core? I believe we should begin by taking an honest look at our routine business activities (see "The Moral Stepladder," p. 36–37). To what degree do actions, intended to maximize self-interest, interfere with the company's overall interest? Are decisions influenced by political connivance? Does bureaucracy overwhelm individual responsibility? Do rules and procedures take precedence over human judgment, even when the application of the rule to a particular situation is counterproductive or unjust?

Morality is either facilitated or hindered by the environment. People who may be moral at home are often less moral at work because only the most courageous of us can step out of roles and expectations when it feels like everyone else is "selling out." The journey toward moral excellence entails an ongoing ratcheting up of personal moral formation in tandem with creating a culture that supports and expects such practices. I believe that transforming the moral ecology of a corporation entails two broad-gauge strategies: (1) establishing moral principles for human relations in a company, much as financial information is based on accounting principles; and (2) encouraging managers to pursue their personal moral formation with the same vitality with which they develop professional skills.

Guiding Principles

To identify central organizing principles for human behavior, we can rely on much wisdom that has been collected and tested over the centuries. From

THE MORAL STEPLADDER

Transforming an organization's character begins with raising the level of managerial moral behavior in routine matters that are usually invisible to anyone outside a given manager's work environs. It helps me to grasp this abstract notion by envisioning a stepladder for ranking a manager's response to an ordinary day-to-day business situation.

For instance, suppose an employee suggests to his or her manager that a certain standard procedure is wasteful and might be performed more economically by a proposed change. However, the manager believes that such a change would be unpopular with the head of another department, who, in turn, would lobby against it with his boss, so he decides to ignore it. In other words, he puts self-interest ahead of common interest and risk avoidance ahead of his personal responsibility.

The scenario I have described represents behavior on a low rung of our moral stepladder. Nothing done was illegal, nor can anyone point with evidence to a lie. If it were questioned, it would no doubt be excused as something that fell between the cracks. But repeated acts like this sap the vitality of worker teams, stunt the growth of individual aspirations, and tarnish the souls of corporations. They also damage the financial performance of the organization, because it is impossible for dispirited people to thrust themselves fully into productive action for the benefit of an organization of which they are—whether they admit it to themselves or not—ashamed. I label this rung of our moral stepladder, "Putting Self-Interest First."

If we look at the same scenario on the next rung of our moral stepladder, our manager evaluates the employee's suggestion on the basis of how it will affect quality and cost, is not influenced by self-interest or politics, and recommends that it be introduced into operations. His idea may be adopted, but more likely, his original fears were accurate and the suggestion is vetoed for political reasons. He informs the employee who originally made the suggestion and expresses appreciation for his thought and effort. We label this rung, "A Moral Effort Overwhelmed by the System."

(continued on next page)

THE MORAL STEPLADDER, *continued*

The highest rung on our ladder belongs to the manager whose sense of personal responsibility is strong. He attempts to change "the system" from one based on politics to one based on merit. How might he go about this? He could commit himself to adopting the highest rung on the ladder as his personal standard for his area of responsibility. He could then set expectations for his staff that all departmental decisions be executed at the higher step of the ladder. After an example is set in his own department, which no doubt others will notice, he can credibly advocate for change in the larger entity. We might call this step on our moral stepladder, "Marching to My Full Moral Potential (without becoming a fanatic or martyr)."

This simple and fictitious story offers a scale for comparing the relative character of moral action from a low-level approach to an admirable effort. Thinking of moral action in terms of a progression (i.e., using a stepladder) gets people in an organization out of the either/or trap of "It's not immoral, so it's OK."

---

my experience as a business practitioner, I would suggest four basic guiding values: localness, merit, openness, and leanness.

Localness is a philosophy that guides the conduct of relations between different levels in an organization. It is more than just decentralization—it is about liberating employees from the oppressive features of the command-and-control structure so that each individual may use his or her job to stretch his or her talents in ways that also benefit the organization. Localness disperses power to competent people in an orderly, disciplined way. Over the long term, wisely distributed power produces better economic results than does centralized power.

Merit means directing every decision and action toward the organization's goals and aspirations, while being consistent with the company's other values. In practice, merit helps to cure the office politics and proliferation of bureaucracy that can demean the dignity of people engaged in work.

Openness and honesty are the world's best navigational instruments. These qualities enable an institution or individual to take stock of where they are, and to chart a course for where they want to go.

Leanness tempers the human inclination for excess comfort and expansion, so that an organization or individual will maintain its health in both good and poor economic times. It embeds the ancient virtue of thrift into the soul of the corporation.

Another foundational principle, which I believe underlies the four values stated above, is love. I am not referring here to the romantic or familial connotations of the word, but to "love" in its most universal meaning: extending one's self toward helping another person to become complete. In this sense, love is a predisposition toward helping our employees, customers, vendors, owners, or other constituents. It is an attitude that we can cultivate and direct by our will, just as we do with other personality characteristics. The central question to ask oneself in putting the value of love into practice in the workplace is, "What can I do to help Joe or Mary (or ten thousand employees) complete themselves more fully as human beings?"

Practicing the value of love in business is not a soft undertaking, nor is it without tension. The loving manager is always faced with the pressure of achieving the business imperative—balancing the common good of the organization with the needs of the individual. Oftentimes, rendering that help requires inflicting short-term hurt, such as telling someone things he or she would rather not hear. Have no illusions—delivering or receiving this kind of message is not fun. But when it is done for the purpose of assisting in growth, it is a loving act. And if it is genuinely intended, it will be heard and appreciated, even when it hurts. If a loving manager is quick and tough in addressing issues when they surface, most damaging organizational issues can be kept at a minimal level.

Moral Formation of Managers

In order to embed these guiding principles in our workplace, we must cultivate value-based relationships, particularly between individuals at different echelons. This leads us to the second aspect of creating a culture based on moral excellence: promoting the moral development of managers. Those who have highest operating responsibility in an organization should have an equal responsibility for their own moral formation. I believe that when a company engages a manager in a leadership position, his character is as important a consideration as his professional competency.

The emphasis on the importance of promoting the moral formation of mangers is not meant to imply that the majority of managers are immoral. That has not been my experience in more than 35 years in corporate life. But I do believe that most managers operate in a system where morality is underdeveloped in relation to professional skills in technology, finance, communications, etc. Many managers do not achieve the excellence they are capable of, simply because they have not devoted enough time to reflecting on the application of the wisdom of the ages to their professional responsibilities.

Leaders who intend to build corporations that tap into the full inner resources of their people must pay as much attention to their own moral formation and that of their key managers as they do to mental and technical proficiency. As an individual assumes more responsibility in the organization, moral formation becomes even more important. The depth of commitment that employees make to the company's well-being is directly related to their perception of the moral formation of their boss and their boss's bosses. The same can be said to a lesser degree about a customer's loyalty to a supplier.

When a board of directors removes a CEO because the company doesn't respond to his direction, or when a leader loses his position of power because his followers reject him (as happened to Richard Nixon), those who have known the deposed individual frequently say, "Success didn't change him. It *unmasked* him."

Behind that comment is the tacit belief that the individual had some chinks in his character all along, but he was still able to perform his responsibilities competently and move on to even higher levels in the company. But what are minor cracks in moral formation in upper middle management positions can be fatal flaws in senior managers, because they set the moral tone for the organization as a whole. This is a critical point that is often underestimated by those with the responsibility for anointing senior executives or CEOs and by those preparing themselves for higher responsibility.

Leadership Qualities

Creating a culture based on moral excellence requires a commitment among managers to embody and develop two qualities in their leadership: virtue and wisdom. The dictionary defines virtue as "moral excellence; right living; goodness." Virtue comes from the Latin word *virtus*, which means "manliness," or "virility." Yet, in modern management circles, virtue is often associated with notions of softness and weakness. Let there be no doubt, transforming corporate rat races into morally uplifting cultures that earn superior financial returns requires an inner toughness on the part of leaders—a willingness to stand against the crowd, an ability to question well-rationalized assumptions, and a faith in the power of the human spirit.

Wisdom, in turn, is more than intelligence. It suggests a special quality of judgment in human affairs, based on knowledge of moral principles, human nature, human needs, and human values. Wisdom is more than what people know, it is who they have become; and who they have become is determined by how congruent their behavior is with their knowledge.

Getting from Here to There

Creating a values-based organization is a formidable undertaking. This is true whether you are the CEO of a complex corporation with 100,000 employees or the manager of a small, autonomous division. It is a lifetime's work, and with each step forward, there are new obstacles to overcome and new risks to be taken. Just as your organization reaches one plateau, a new mountain will emerge on the horizon.

It took Jack Adam (my predecessor as CEO at Hanover) and myself six years to see the link between the changes we made in our governance structure and the improved economic performance that followed. It took us an additional six years to build what we considered a mature, values-based, vision-driven culture—meaning our experiment in corporate governance reached a point where it produced consistently superior financial results and widely recognizable individual growth through a process that we knew how to replicate.

Why does it take so long? Because in order to bring about such a transformation, management has to change some of its long-held mental models

CHALLENGING OUR MENTAL MODELS

The cultural shift toward moral excellence will require rethinking our old mental models, and developing new paradigms for corporate life. The following are several shifts that I see occurring:

Work is viewed as a platform on which people mature and achieve happiness by developing their competencies as well as contributing to the Gross World Product. As an employee, a person is *first* a human being and *second* an instrument of production. When workers sense this fundamental order in a company, they will devote considerable energy to achieving the company's business goals.

Corporate Ecologies based on values and visions (aspirations) will generally outperform command-and-control corporations.

Learning exclusively through the mechanical, reductionistic model has served business well up to now. But it must be augmented by systemic understanding of the enormous interconnectedness in our world.

Leadership in a vision-driven, value-guided organization has a high component of service, learning, and love. It is about building character and advancing learning throughout the organization.

and replace long-standing habits (see "Challenging Our Mental Models"). People quickly grasp the intellectual dimension of these ideas, and the overwhelming majority, in my experience, conceptually agree with them. But internalizing the ideas and translating them into practice takes quite a bit longer. There needs to be debate and discussion, as individuals wrestle with the personal implications of the new ideas. These conversations will then be followed by the application of the concepts to authentic situations.

Take a Look Inside

Embedding a new philosophy in an organization consists of a series of small successes, followed by bigger successes. All the while, management must live up to the philosophy—in both good times as well as times of crisis. In other words, people must see that the new philosophy works better than the culture being phased out, and also see that their manager is "walking the talk." While this progress is taking place, there will be periods of skepticism and times of enthusiasm, periods of doubt and times of confidence.

Ultimately, the quest for organizational transformation must begin with a personal commitment within each individual to pursue moral excellence. Pushing for the transformation of an organization's culture entails risk, and we can face that risk only if we are clear about our convictions and the beliefs we want to live by. It comes back to Gandhi's observation that transformation takes place when you "become the change that you wish to see in the world."

Although this type of cultural change will take time, the potential payoff is immense. The benefits of releasing bottled-up human energy through the pursuit of moral excellence will show up in a tremendous increase in productivity, as well as unimagined improvements in relationships with external constituencies, who will respond positively to the quality of the experiences they have with such an organization.

It has been my experience that when people are free to choose between high-quality ideas or inferior ones, they inevitably choose the former. They deserve to have this choice in our corporations. ☞

This article is an edited version of B. O'Brien, "Moral Formation for Managers: Closing the Gap Between Intention and Practice" (Cambridge, MA: MIT Center for Organizational Learning Research Monograph, 1995). Copyright © 1995 by Bill O'Brien.

Bill O'Brien was the chief executive officer of Hanover Insurance Company until his retirement in 1991. During his 21-year tenure at Hanover, Bill coauthored a business philosophy that resulted in a significant corporate turnaround. By applying the concepts of organizational learning, he and his staff created one of the most respected companies in the insurance industry, both in terms of the work environment and its profitability.

—

Chapter Four

Rethinking Leadership in the Learning Organization

by Peter M. Senge

"**N**o significant change will occur unless it is driven from the top." "There's no point in starting a change process unless the CEO is on board." "Nothing will happen without top management buy-in."

How many times have we heard statements like these and simply accepted them as "the way things are"? CEOs and other top executives talk about the need to "transform" their organizations, to overthrow stodgy bureaucratic cultures, and to "become learning organizations." But evidence of successful corporate transformations is meager. Moreover, the basic assumption that only top management can cause significant change is deeply disempowering. Why, then, do we accept it so unquestioningly? Isn't it odd that we should seek to bring about less authoritarian cultures by resorting to hierarchical authority?

Perhaps there is an element of self-protection at work—the comfort of being able to hold someone else (namely, top management) responsible for the lack of effective leadership. There is no doubt that a CEO who is opposed to fundamental change can make life difficult for internal innovators, but this hardly proves that only the CEO can bring about significant change.

43

Two Views on Leadership

Let's consider some *different* statements about leadership and change: "Little significant change can occur *if* it is driven from the top." "CEO proclamations and programs rolled out from corporate headquarters are a good way to undermine deeper changes." "Top-management 'buy-in' is a poor substitute for genuine commitment at many levels in an organization."

These statements are supported by the experiences of two innovative leaders, Phil Carroll of Shell Oil and Rich Teerlink of Harley-Davidson. As Phil Carroll recalled, "When I first came in as CEO, everyone thought, 'Phil will tell us what he wants us to do.' But I didn't have a clue, and if I had, it would have been a disaster." Likewise, Rich Teerlink said, "Anyone who thinks the CEO can drive this kind of change is wrong."

There are several reasons why leaders like Carroll and Teerlink have come to a more humble view of the power of top management. First is the cynicism that exists in most organizations after years of management fads. When the CEO preaches about "becoming a learning organization," people roll their eyes and think to themselves, "Here we go again. I wonder what seminar s/he went to last weekend." Most corporations have had so many "flavor-of-the-month" initiatives from management that people immediately discount any new pronouncement as more "executive cheerleading" or, as they say at Harley-Davidson, "another fine program."

A second reason has to do with the difference between compliance and commitment. Hierarchical authority is much more effective at securing compliance than it is in fostering genuine commitment. "It seemed that every year someone pressured us to change our promotion review process to incorporate our values," reflects former Hanover Insurance CEO Bill O'Brien. "But we never caved in to this pressure. A value is only a value if it is voluntarily chosen. No reward system has ever been invented that people in an organization haven't learned how to 'game.' We didn't want just new behaviors. We wanted new behaviors for the right reasons" (see "Transforming the Character of a Corporation," p. 33). There is simply no substitute for commitment in bringing about deep change. No one can force another person to learn, especially if that learning involves deep changes in beliefs and attitudes or fundamentally new ways of thinking and acting.

A third reason a different type of leadership is needed is that top-management initiatives often end up moving organizations backward, not forward. This can occur in obvious ways, such as top-management downsizings and reorganizations that have the side-effect of increasing internal competitiveness, which ends up undermining collaboration and, ultimately, economic performance. But it can also occur more subtly, even in changes explicitly designed to improve learning. For example, a mandated "360-degree feedback" process not only reinforces a compliance mentality, but it also lessens the likelihood of people surfacing what Harvard's Chris Argyris called the "potentially embarrassing information" that might "produce real change" ("Good Communication That Blocks Real Learning," *Harvard Business Review*, July/August 1994). This kind of information will come into the open only when people have genuine trust, curiosity, and shared responsibility—conditions not usually fostered by mandated programs.

Even so, it must be acknowledged that many large-scale change programs—reorganizations, downsizing, corporate-wide cost reduction programs, or re-engineering programs—can be implemented only from top-management levels. But such changes will not affect the corporate culture if it is based on fear and defensiveness. Nor will they unleash people's imagination and passions and enhance their ability to form genuinely shared visions. They will not change the quality of thinking in the organization, or increase intelligence at the front lines, where people confront increasingly complex and dynamic business environments. And they will do nothing to foster the trust and skills needed by teams at all levels if they are to reflect on hidden assumptions and to inquire into the reasoning behind their own actions.

Types of Leadership

For the past 20 years, many colleagues and I have been working with managers and teams to develop enhanced learning capabilities that center around five related disciplines: systems thinking, surfacing and improving mental models, fostering dialogue, nurturing personal vision, and building shared visions. A group of us at MIT formed a consortium of corporations, The Center for Organizational Learning, with two main objectives: to advance the theory and method underlying this work; and to demonstrate what is possible when organizations begin working together toward integrating new learning capabilities into important work settings.

Most corporations have had so many "flavor-of-the-month" initiatives from management that people immediately discount any new pronouncement as more "executive cheerleading" or, as they say at Harley-Davidson, "another fine program."

Within these companies, we regularly confronted the dilemmas posed by the conflicting views of leadership described above. Resolving these dilemmas, however, required fundamental shifts in our traditional thinking about leadership.

These shifts start with the simple view of leaders as those people who "walk ahead," people who are genuinely committed to deep change in themselves and in their organizations and who demonstrate their commitment through their actions. They lead through developing new understandings, new skills, and new capabilities for individual and collective learning. And they come from many places within an organization.

In particular, we identified three essential types of leaders in building learning organizations, roughly corresponding to three different organizational positions:

1. *Local line leaders*, who can undertake meaningful experiments to test whether new learning capabilities actually lead to improved business results.

2. *Executive leaders*, who provide support for line leaders, develop learning infrastructures, and lead by example in the gradual process of evolving the norms and behaviors of a learning culture.

3. *Internal networkers*, or *community builders*, who can move freely about the organization to find those who are predisposed to bringing about change, to help out in organizational experiments, and to aid in the diffusion of new learning.

Local Line Leaders

Nothing can start without committed local line leaders: individuals with significant business responsibility and "bottom-line" focus. They head organizational units that are microcosms of the larger organization, and yet have enough autonomy to be able to undertake meaningful change independent of the larger organization. To create useful experiments, they must confront the same issues and business challenges that are occurring within the larger organization. For example, a unique cross-functional task force may be less useful for a learning experiment than a team that manages a process that is ongoing, generic, and vital for future competitiveness, such as a product development team, a sales team, or a business division.

The key role played by local line leaders is to sanction significant practical experiments and to lead through active participation in those experiments. Without serious experiments aimed at connecting new learning capabilities to business results, there is no way to assess whether enhancing learning capabilities is just an intellectually appealing idea or if it can really make a difference. Typically, an MIT Learning Center project began with a core team composed of line leaders who initially worked together for six to twelve months. During this time, they worked on developing their own skills in systems thinking, collaborative inquiry, and building shared vision, and then began applying those skills to their own issues. Only then did they began designing learning processes that might spread such skills throughout their organization and become embedded in how work was done.

For example, a team of sales managers and sales representatives at Federal Express worked together for over a year before they began to develop what eventually became the Global Customer Learning Laboratory. "We felt we needed new tools for working with our key corporate customers as learning partners," said Cathy Stopcynski of Federal Express. "That's why the Global Customer Learning Laboratory is important. It gives us a whole new way to work together with customers to improve our collective thinking and come up with completely new solutions to complex logistics problems." At Electronic Data Systems (EDS), a growing network of local line leaders brought learning organization principles and methods into work with customers through EDS's "Leading Learning Communities" program.

In addition to playing a key role in the design and implementation of new learning processes, local line leaders often become teachers once these learning processes become established. In fact, the most effective facilitators in learning processes such as the Global Customer Learning Laboratory are usually not professional trainers but the line managers themselves. Their substantive knowledge and practical experience give them unique credibility. Facilitating others' learning is also a powerful, ongoing way for line leaders to deepen their own understanding and capabilities.

However, engaging local line leaders may be difficult. As pragmatists, they often find ideas like systems thinking, mental models, and dialogue intangible and "hard to get their hands around." "When I was first exposed to the MIT work," said Fred Simon, former head of the Lincoln Continental program at Ford Motor Company, "I was highly skeptical. I had heard so many 'academic' theories that made sense but never produced for us. But I was also not happy with our team's ability to work together. I knew there must be a better way, and my business planning manager was convinced this could make a difference."

Simon's view is typical of many line leaders at the outset: He was skeptical, but he recognized that he had problems that he could not solve. He also had a trusted colleague who was willing to engage with him. Again and again, we have found that healthy, open-minded skeptics can become the most effective leaders and, eventually, champions of this work. They keep the horse in front of the cart by focusing first and foremost on business results. Such people invariably have more staying power than the "fans" who get excited about new ideas but whose excitement wanes once the newness wears off.

Because line leaders are focused primarily on their business unit, however, they may not think much about learning within the larger organization, and typically they have little time to devote to diffusion of their efforts. They may also be unaware of—and relatively inept at dealing with—the anti-learning forces in the larger organization. They become impatient when the larger organization does not change to match their new ideas, and may start to feel misunderstood and unappreciated. They can easily develop an "us against the world" mentality, which will make them especially ineffective in communicating their ideas to others.

> **But the "better mousetrap" theory may not apply in large institutions. Improved results are often threatening to others, and the more dramatic the improvement, the greater the threat.**

Innovative local line managers are often more at risk than they realize. They typically believe, "My bosses will leave me alone as long as I produce results, regardless of the methods I use." But the "better mousetrap" theory may not apply in large institutions. Improved results are often threatening to others, and the more dramatic the improvement, the greater the threat. Large organizations have complex forces that maintain the status quo and inhibit the spread of new ideas. Often, even the most effective local line leaders fail to understand these forces or know how to work with them.

Despite these limitations, committed local line leadership is essential. At least half of the MIT Learning Center companies that made significant strides in improving business results and developing internal learning capabilities had little or no executive leadership. But we saw *no* examples where significant progress was made in an organization without leadership from local line managers, and many examples where sincerely committed CEOs failed to generate any significant momentum.

Executive Leaders

At the Learning Center, our excitement around the practical experiments led by local line managers frequently made us blind to the necessary and complementary roles played by executive leaders. Local line leaders *can* benefit significantly from "executive champions" who can be protectors, mentors, and thinking partners. When dramatic improvements achieved in one line organization threaten others, executive partners can help manage the threat. Alternatively, executive partners can make sure that new innovative practices are not ignored because people are too busy to take the time to understand what the innovators are doing. By working in concert with internal networkers, executives can help connect innovative local line leaders with other like-minded people. They also play a mentoring role in helping the local line leaders understand complex political cross-currents and communicate their ideas and accomplishments to those who have not been involved.

In one company, a local line organization had achieved what it regarded as dramatic improvements in the product development process, but its efforts lacked credibility when judged by more traditional metrics. For instance, at critical checkpoints the team had record numbers of engineering change orders. The team interpreted this as evidence that people were more willing to surface and fix problems early in the development process. But outside the team, these same orders were seen as evidence that the group was "out of control." Eventually, executives in the company commissioned an independent audit, which showed that the team was indeed highly effective. The executives also supported the development of a "learning history" to help others understand how the team had accomplished its results.

Part of our difficulty with appreciating the role that effective executive leadership can play in learning is that all of us are used to the "captain of the ship" image of traditional hierarchical leaders. However, when executives act as teachers, stewards, and designers, they fill roles that are much more subtle, contextual, and long term than the traditional model of the power-wielding hierarchical leader.

"We in top management are responsible for creating an operating environment that can allow continual learning," said Harley-Davidson's Teerlink. Although executive leadership has traditionally focused on structure and strategy, Teerlink and other executives are increasingly thinking about the operating environment in less tangible ways.

Effective executive leaders can build an environment that is conducive to learning in several ways. The first is by articulating *guiding ideas*. "I have always believed that good ideas will drive out bad ideas," said Hanover's O'Brien. "One of the basic problems with business today is that our organizations are guided by too many mediocre ideas—ideas which do not foster aspirations worthy of people's commitment." Guiding ideas are different from slogans or management buzzwords. They are developed gradually, often over many years, through reflection on an organization's history and traditions and on its long-term growth and opportunities.

A second way to build operating environments for learning is through conscious attention to *learning infrastructure*. In a world of rapid change and increasing interdependence, learning is too important to be left to chance. I have met many CEOs in recent years who have lamented that "we can't learn from ourselves" or "we are better at learning from competitors than from our own people." But with little or no infrastructure to support ongoing learning, one might ask, "Why *should* successful new practices spread in organizations?" Who studies these innovations to document why they worked? Where are the learning processes that will enable others to follow in the footsteps of successful innovators? Who is responsible for creating these learning processes?

There can be little doubt of the long-term business impact of executive leadership in developing learning infrastructure. When the Royal Dutch/Shell Group's central group planning leaders became convinced that "scenario thinking" was a vital survival skill in turbulent, unpredictable world oil markets, they didn't initiate a set of scenario-planning courses for Shell's management. Instead, they redesigned the planning infrastructure so that management teams regularly were asked not just for their budget and their "plan," but for several plans describing how they would manage under multiple possible futures. "Planning as learning" gradually became a way of life within Shell—a change to which many attribute Shell's rise to preeminence in the world oil business.

A third way to build operating environments for learning lies within the executive's own domain for taking action—namely, the *executive team* itself. It is important that executives recognize that they, too, must change, and that many of the skills that have made them successful in the past can actually inhibit learning.

I think these ideas will eventually lead to a very different mind-set and, ultimately, a different skill-set among executives. "Gradually, I have come to see a whole new model for my role as a CEO," said Shell Oil's Carroll. "Perhaps my real job is to be the *ecologist for the organization.* We must learn how to see the company as a living system and to see it as a system within the context of the larger systems of which it is a part. Only then will our vision reliably include return for our shareholders, a productive environment for our employees, and a social vision for the company as a whole."

Internal Networkers

The most unappreciated leadership role is that of the internal networkers, or what we often call internal community builders. Internal networkers are effective for the very reasons that top-management efforts to initiate change can backfire—oftentimes, no power *is* power. Precisely because they have no positional authority, internal networkers are free to move about a large organization relatively unnoticed.

When the CEO visits someone, everyone knows. When the CEO says, "We need to become a learning organization," everyone nods. But when someone with little or no positional authority begins asking which people are genuinely interested in changing the way they and their teams work, the only ones likely to respond are those who are genuinely interested. And if the internal networker finds one person who is interested and asks, "Who else do you think really cares about these things?" he or she is likely to receive an honest response. The only authority possessed by internal networkers comes from the strength of their convictions and the clarity of their ideas.

It is very difficult to identify the internal networkers because they can be people in many different organizational positions. They might be internal consultants, trainers, or personnel staff in organization development or human resources. They might be front-line workers like engineers, sales representatives, or shop stewards. They might, under some circumstances, be in senior staff positions. What is important is that they are able to move around the organization freely, with high accessibility to many parts of the organization. They understand the informal networks through which information and stories flow and how innovative practices naturally diffuse within organizations.

Internal networkers are effective for the very reasons that top-management efforts to initiate change can backfire—oftentimes no power is power. . . . The only authority possessed by internal networkers comes from the strength of their convictions and the clarity of their ideas.

The first vital function played by internal networkers is to identify local line managers who have the power to take action and who are predisposed to developing new learning capabilities. Much time and energy can be wasted by working with the wrong people, especially in the early stages of a change process. Convincing people that they should be interested in systems thinking or learning is inherently a low-leverage strategy. Even if they are persuaded initially, they are unlikely to persevere.

When the liaison officers from the Learning Center companies were asked how they each got started in this work, they responded, virtually unanimously, that they were "predisposed." All of them had something in their backgrounds—perhaps an especially influential college course, a particular work experience, or just lifelong interest—that made them more open to the systems perspective. They each had a deep curiosity about learning, or mental models, or the mystery of profound teamwork. In turn, they felt attuned to others they met who shared this predisposition.

In ongoing experiments within line organizations, we have found that internal networkers can help in many ways. In Learning Center projects, they served as project managers, as co-facilitators, or as "learning histori-ans"—people trained to track a major change process and to help those who are involved to better reflect on what they are learning (see "Learning Histories: 'Assessing' the Learning Organization," *The Systems Thinker*, May 1995). As practical knowledge is built, internal networkers continue to serve as organizational "seed carriers," connecting like-minded people from diverse settings and making them aware of each other's learning efforts. Gradually, they may help in developing the more formal coordination and steering mechanisms needed to move from local experiments to broader, organization-wide learning. At Ford, for example, an informal "Leaders of Learning" group was formed by local line leaders and internal networkers who wanted to share learnings and serve as a strategic leadership body. They saw their work as supporting continuing experiments, connecting those experiments with the interests of top management, and wrestling with orga-nization-wide capacity building and learning.

As with local line managers and executive leaders, the limitations of internal networkers are likewise counterparts to their strengths. Because they do not have a great deal of formal authority, they can do little to counter hierarchical authority directly. If a local line leader becomes a threat to peers or supervisors, they may be powerless to help him or her. Internal networkers have no authority to institute changes in organizational structures or processes. So, even though they are essential, internal net-workers are most effective when working in concert with local line leaders and executive leaders.

The Leadership Challenges

The leadership challenges inherent in building learning organizations are a microcosm of the leadership issue of our times: how human communities can productively confront complex issues where hierarchical authority is inade-quate to bring about change. None of today's most pressing issues—deterio-ration of the natural environment, the international arms race, erosion of the public education system, or the breakdown of the family and increasing social fragmentation—will be resolved through hierarchical authority.

In all these issues, there are no single causes, no simple "fixes." There is no one villain to blame. There will be no magic pill. Significant change will require imagination, perseverance, dialogue, deep caring, and a willingness to change on the part of millions of people. I believe these same challenges exist in the work of building learning organizations.

In 1995, a group of CEOs from the Learning Center companies spent a half-day with Karl-Henrik Robèrt, the founder of Sweden's path-breaking Natural Step process for helping societies become ecologically sustainable. The next day, Rich Teerlink of Harley-Davidson came in and said, "I don't know why I stay awake at night trying to figure out how to transform a six-thousand person company. Yesterday, we talked with someone who is transforming a country of four million people."

The necessity of creating systemic change where hierarchy is inadequate will, I believe, push us to new views of leadership based on new principles. These challenges cannot be met by isolated heroic leaders. They will require a unique mix of different people, in different positions, who lead in different ways. Although the picture sketched above is tentative and will certainly evolve over time, I doubt that it understates the changes that will be required in our traditional leadership models. ⟿

This article is an edited version of P. Senge, "Leading Learning Organizations" (Cambridge, MA: MIT Center for Organizational Learning Research Monograph, 1995). Copyright © 1995 by Peter M. Senge. It has also appeared in the Peter F. Drucker Foundation book *The Leader of the Future*, M. Goldsmith, F. Hesselbein, and R. Beckhard, eds. (San Francisco: Jossey-Bass, 1995). In 1997 the MIT Center for Organizational Learning became the new Society for Organizational Learning (SoL).

Peter M. Senge is a senior lecturer at the Massachusetts Institute of Technology, where he is part of the Organizational Learning and Change group. He is also chairman of the Society for Organizational Learning. He is the author of the widely acclaimed book *The Fifth Discipline: The Art and Practice of the Learning Organization*, and, with colleagues Charlotte Roberts, Rick Ross, Bryan Smith, and Art Kleiner, coauthor of *The Fifth Discipline Fieldbook: Strategies and Tools for Building a Learning Organization*.

≈⌒

Envisioning
and
Building
Learning
Communities

As with any change effort, building learning communities will remain only a vision unless we share our ideas for how to make that vision real. Part Three of The New Workplace *presents five articles that address several key issues related to implementation.*

In "Can Learning Cultures Evolve?" Edgar H. Schein starts things off by examining the nature of learning—and the typical roadblocks that we face in trying to move generative change forward. Schein takes an especially close look at the complex effects anxiety can have on learning.

In "The Inner Game of Work: Building Capability in the Workplace," Tim Gallwey discusses personal assumptions that often stand in the way of learning. He then shows how revealing those very assumptions can be a crucial first step in maximizing individual potential. Finally, he proposes an intriguing new role—the leader as coach—as a way to promote learning.

The third chapter in this section, "Creating a New Workplace: Making a Commitment to Community," offers nine disciplines for moving a company's culture closer to community. The author, Greg Zlevor, argues that we need to see community building as a journey rather than a specific, unchanging condition that we must strive to maintain at all times. Zlevor contrasts community with what he calls "dis-ciety," and shows how these two conditions form a continuum along which companies may migrate.

In "Building a Core Competence in Community," Kaz Gozdz explores how efforts to preserve a cherished spirit of community can actually destroy it instead—if we ignore the nature of that spirit. Echoing Greg Zlevor's theme about the fragile nature of community, Gozdz then shows how a sense of community can ebb and flow with the life cycle of a company. He concludes with suggestions for enhancing collective intelligence, establishing a "learning architecture," and sustaining community as it matures through various natural stages of growth.

The final piece in this section—"The Learning Organization Journey: Assessing and Valuing Progress," by Nils Bohlin and Paul Brenner—addresses the vital question of how we know our organization is becoming a learning community. The authors recommend assessing three key areas: knowledge base, learning practices, and learning climate. They then offer guidelines for assessing learning, and make a strong argument for establishing ongoing assessment practices.

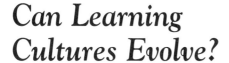

Chapter Five

Can Learning
Cultures Evolve?

by Edgar H. Schein

There is much agreement that one of the key characteristics of the 21st-century organization will be its ongoing ability to learn. In fact, it has been said that the ability to learn will be a major competitive advantage for organizations. These beliefs have generated a frenzy of activity in recent years, as business leaders scramble to figure out not only what organizational learning is, but how to do it.

These activities perhaps contain more optimism than realism. Learning is, at its heart, a complex and difficult process—a source of joy when it works, but a source of pain and tension when it does not. Learning forces us to fundamentally rethink the way we view the world—a process that is difficult in part because our cultural assumptions predispose us to take certain things for granted, rather than to re-examine them continually. Since learning and culture are so closely interrelated, it is incumbent upon us to understand more about the interaction of the two, and to identify, if possible, what elements of a culture might truly facilitate learning to learn.

Two Kinds of Learning

To understand the important role that organizational culture plays in learning, we need to first make a distinction between two types of learning: "adaptive" and "generative." (The term "generative learning" comes from

Peter Senge. However, the same process has been labeled by Chris Argyris and Donald Schön as "double-loop learning," while Don Michael, Gregory Bateson, and others have identified it as "learning how to learn.")

Adaptive learning is usually a fairly straightforward process. We identify a problem or a gap between where we are and where we want to be, and we set about to solve the problem and close the gap. Generative learning, on the other hand, comes into play when we discover that the identification of the problem or gap itself is contingent on learning new ways of perceiving and thinking about our problems (i.e., rethinking cultural assumptions and norms).

For example, from an adaptive point of view, we may decide that we have to replace corporate hierarchies with flat networks in order to reduce costs and increase coordination. From a generative point of view, however, we might instead begin by examining our mental models and considering how hierarchies and networks might be integrated into a more effective corporate design. From "either this or that" thinking, we might have to develop the capacity to think about "this and that."

Two Kinds of Anxiety

The very process of identifying problems, seeing new possibilities, and changing the routines by which we adapt or cope requires rethinking and redesign, because we have to unlearn some things before new things can be learned. Thus, generative learning, by its very nature, asks us to question our mental models, our personal ways of thinking and acting, and our relationships with each other. This deep level of change can produce two kinds of anxiety.

The first is the fear of something new. Instability or unpredictability is uncomfortable and arouses anxiety—what I have called "Change Anxiety," or the fear of changing—based on a fear of the unknown. Adaptive learning, whether it be in individuals, groups, or organizations, tends toward stability. We seek to institutionalize those things that work. Indeed, it is the stable routines and habits of thought and perception that we call "culture." We seek novelty only when most of our surroundings are stable and under control.

However, learning how to learn may require deliberately seeking out unstable, less predictable, and possibly less meaningful situations. It may also require perpetual learning, which opens up the possibility of being continually subject to Change Anxiety. This is a situation most of us would prefer to avoid.

But if, as many people anticipate, the economic, political, technological, and sociocultural global environment will itself become more turbulent and unpredictable, then new problems will constantly emerge and past solutions will constantly become inadequate. This brings us to a second type of anxiety, which I call "Survival Anxiety"—the uncomfortable realization that in order to survive and thrive, we must change.

In order for learning to occur, somehow we must reach a psychological point where the fear of not learning (Survival Anxiety) is greater than the fear associated with entering the unknown and unpredictable (Change Anxiety).

As teachers, coaches, and managers, how then do we make sure that Survival Anxiety is greater than Change Anxiety? One method is to increase Survival Anxiety until the fear of not changing is so great that it overwhelms the fear of changing. We can do this by threatening the learner in various ways, or by providing strong incentives for learning. For example, if employees feel that they will not get promoted in the organization if they don't use electronic mail or conduct their meetings with the latest groupware, it would seem logical that they would want to keep up with new technology.

However, humans don't always do what logic dictates. If an employee's Change Anxiety becomes too high, he or she may instead become defensive, misperceive the situation, deny reality, or rationalize his or her current behavior. Change agents often come up against this type of resistance to organizational change and retreat to the rationalization that "it's simply human to resist change."

Perhaps a more effective way to initiate change is to reduce Change Anxiety so that it is less than Survival Anxiety. We can do this by concentrating on making the learner feel more comfortable about the learning process, about trying new things, and about entering the perpetual unknown (see "Reducing Change Anxiety," p. 62).

REDUCING CHANGE ANXIETY

How do we focus on and actually reduce Change Anxiety? How do we make learning a safe and desirable process? I believe there are at least eight conditions that must be created in order to allow this to happen:

1. Provide psychological safety—a sense that something new will not . cause loss of identity or of our sense of competence.

2. Provide a vision of a better future that makes it worthwhile to experience risk and tolerate pain.

3. Provide a practice field where it is acceptable to make mistakes and learn from them.

4. Provide direction and guidance for learning, to help the learner get started.

5. Start the learning process in groups, so learners can share their feelings of anxiety and help each other cope.

6. Provide coaching by teaching basic skills and giving feedback during practice periods.

7. Reward even the smallest steps toward learning.

8. Provide a climate in which making mistakes or errors is seen as being in the interest of learning—so that, as Don Michael has so eloquently noted, we come to embrace errors because they enable us to learn.

Addressing the anxiety caused by learning and change is certainly a good way to begin the learning process, at least at the individual and small group levels. But how can we apply the generative learning process across various organizational boundaries and sustain the learning process over longer periods of time? This requires the creation of an organizational culture that supports perpetual learning at the individual, group, and organizational levels.

A Learning Culture

What would such a culture look like? Learning cultures share at least seven basic elements:

1. A concern for people, which takes the form of an equal concern for all of the company's stakeholders—customers, employees, suppliers, the community, and stockholders. No one group dominates management's thinking because it is recognized that any one group can slow down or destroy the organization.

2. A belief that people can and will learn. It takes a certain amount of idealism about human nature to create a learning culture.

3. A shared belief that people have the capacity to change their environment, and that they ultimately make their own fate. If we believe that the world around us cannot be changed, what is the point of learning to learn?

4. Some amount of slack time available for generative learning, and enough diversity in the people, groups, and subcultures to provide creative alternatives. "Lean and mean" is not a good prescription for organizational learning.

5. A shared commitment to open and extensive communication. This does not mean that all channels in a fully connected network must be used all the time, but it does mean that such channels must be available and the organization must have spent time developing a common vocabulary so that communication can occur.

6. A shared commitment to learning to think systemically in terms of multiple forces, events being over-determined, short- and long-term consequences, feedback loops, and other systemic phenomena. Linear cause-and-effect thinking will prevent accurate diagnosis and, therefore, undermine learning.

7. Interdependent coordination and cooperation. As interdependence increases, the need for teamwork increases. Therefore, organizations must share a belief that teams can and will be effective, and that individualistic competition is not the answer to all questions.

Inhibitors to Learning

Culture is about shared mental models—shared ways of perceiving the world, sorting out that information, reacting to it, and ultimately understanding it. Therefore, in order to understand what prevents us from creating learning cultures, we need to explore the shared assumptions that act as inhibitors to learning. If we look at Western (particularly U.S.) organizational and managerial cultures, there are several shared assumptions or myths that prevent organizations from developing the kind of learning culture I have described (see "Cultural Inhibitors to Learning," p. 64).

CULTURAL INHIBITORS TO LEARNING

- Myth that leaders have to be in control, decisive, and dominant
- Myth of "rugged individualism"
- Shared belief in managerial prerogatives—the "divine rights of managers"
- Belief that power is "the ability not to have to learn anything"
- Achievement as the primary source of status in society
- Compartmentalization of work from family and self
- Belief that task issues should override relationship concerns
- Myth that management is about "hard" things (money, data, "the bottom line") versus "soft" issues (people, groups, and relationships)
- Bias toward linear, short-term thinking versus systemic, long-term thinking

---

Human history has left us with a legacy of patriarchy and hierarchy, and a myth of the "superiority" of our leaders based on the view of the leader as warrior and protector. This has created almost a state of "arrested development" in our organizations, in the sense that we have very limited models of how humans can and should relate to each other in organizational settings. The traditional hierarchical model is virtually the only one we have.

One consequence of this rigid model is that managers start with a self-image of needing to be completely in control—decisive, certain, and dominant. Neither the leader nor the follower wants the leader to be uncertain, to admit to not knowing or not being in control, or to embrace error rather than to defensively deny it. Of course, in reality leaders know that they do not have all of the answers, but few are willing to admit it. And since subordinates demand a public sense of certainty from their leaders, they reinforce this facade. Yet if organizational learning is to occur, leaders themselves must become learners, and in that process, begin to acknowledge their own vulnerability and uncertainty.

In the U.S., we have the additional cultural myth of "rugged individualism" that makes the lone problem-solver the hero. The interdependent, cooperative team player is not typically viewed as a "hero." In fact, compe-

tition between organizational members is viewed as natural and desirable, as a way to identify talent ("the cream will rise to the top"). After all, if teamwork were more natural, would it be such a popular topic in organization development literature? For the most part, teamwork is viewed as a practical necessity, not an intrinsically desirable condition.

Another myth that has developed among managerial circles might be called the "divine rights of managers." Management is believed to have certain prerogatives and obligations that are intrinsic and are, in a sense, the reward for having worked oneself up into the management ranks. The relatively young and egalitarian social structure of the U.S. exacerbates this problem by emphasizing achievement over formal status. We have no clear class structure that provides people with a clear position in society. Hence, they often rely instead on earned position, title, and visible status symbols (cars, homes, etc.) as a way of displaying rank. The competition-based work hierarchy then ultimately becomes the main source of security and status, and higher level managers are expected to act in a more decisive and controlling manner to express that status.

Another barrier to learning is the fact that work roles and tasks are very compartmentalized in the U.S., and are separated from family and self-development concerns. These roles are expected to be treated in an emotionally neutral and objective manner, which makes it very hard to examine the pros and cons of organizational practices that put more emphasis on relationships and feelings. Even talking about anxiety in the workplace is often taboo. This creates an inherent dilemma: How can we effectively address learning-produced anxiety if we cannot discuss it?

Within the work context we have the further problem that task issues are always given primacy over relationship issues. Everyone pays lip service to the notion that people and relationships are important, but our society's basic assumptions are that the real work of managers lies with quantitative data, money, and bottom lines. Within this framework, people can seem like nothing more than another resource to be "deployed" or "controlled." If we have any doubts about the reality of this viewpoint, consider how many performance appraisal systems tend to reduce performance to numbers rather than deal with qualitative descriptions of performance and leadership potential.

The bias toward viewing organizations in quantitative terms shows up most clearly in graduate schools of business, where the popularity of quantitative courses in finance, marketing, and production is much greater than qualitative courses in leadership, group dynamics, or communication. Associated with this myth that management is only about "hard" things is the focus on short time horizons. Driven by our current reporting systems, managers learn early on to pay closer attention to the short-term trends in their financial numbers than to the long-term morale or development of their employees. Creating an environment for learning is a long-range task, yet few managers feel that they have the luxury to plan for people and learning processes.

The combination of this task focus, preference for hard numbers, and short-run orientation all conspire to make systems thinking difficult. Systems are ultimately messy, and they cannot really be understood without taking a longer range point of view, as system dynamics has convincingly demonstrated.

Articulating the Challenge

Creating a learning culture from this set of assumptions is very difficult. It is one thing to specify what it will take for us to become effective learners; it is quite another thing to get there, given these strong cultural inhibitors. But the first and most necessary step is always a frank appraisal of reality. If we understand our cultural biases, we can either set out to overcome them slowly, or, better yet, figure out how to harness them for more effective learning.

But we first must acknowledge the difficulty of our task. Culture is about shared tacit ways of being. Because it operates outside of our awareness, we are often quite ignorant of the degree to which our culture influences us. Therefore, we cannot expect that we can just set about to create whatever culture we want, as if it were the same as creating espoused principles and values. Only shared successes in using a new way of thinking, perceiving, or valuing will create this new approach, and that takes time.

I believe one mechanism by which cultures change is to reprioritize some of the shared assumptions that conflict with others. For example, as we discover that competition and rugged individualism fail in solving important problems, we will experiment more with other forms of organizing and coordinating. Initially we may do it only because it is pragmatically necessary. But gradually we will discover the power of relationships and teams to complete tasks more effectively and to improve learning. This "proactive pragmatism" will eventually force us to create a learning culture and, in that process, produce new and quite different 21st-century organizations. ✑

Edgar H. Schein is Sloan Fellows professor of management emeritus and a senior lecturer at the Sloan School of Management. He is the author of numerous books on organization development.

The Inner Game of Work: Building Capability in the Workplace

by Tim Gallwey

"What would be more interesting to you," I ask an audience of executives, "engaging in a dialogue on learning how to coach or one on learning how to learn?" Generally, 80 to 90 percent of the executives vote for coaching. I point out the obvious—if you learned how to learn, you could apply the knowledge to learning anything, including coaching. And the reverse is not true. So why not learn how to learn?

The answer is usually unspoken but real. Coaching is something I *do* to improve another person or team; it's part of my job. Learning *happens to me*; it makes me feel vulnerable. Learning focuses on my weaknesses, pressuring me to change the way I think and behave. Besides, I'm a professional, with established competencies and knowledge. I'm paid to get results, not to learn.

Thus, managers' most common response to the growing demand for corporations to become learning organizations is to scramble to be the teacher, not the taught—the coach, not the coached. But, to be an effective coach, an individual must understand the nature of learning. And to understand learning, a coach must be actively engaged in the learning process and personally familiar with the kinds of vulnerabilities and obstacles a learner experiences.

Developing Learning Capability

Learning, coaching, and building a learning culture are critical to the success of modern businesses. Because learning increases our ability to perform, the capacity to grow capability is becoming indistinguishable from the capacity to grow wealth. However, unacknowledged resistance to learning and coaching can make it difficult for us to realize the ideals of the learning organization.

As children, we were naturally engaged in learning in everything we did. Thus, as adults, we don't really need to learn how to learn, as much as we need to remember what we once knew. We need to unlearn some of the attitudes and practices we picked up from our formal education that seriously undermine our natural appetite and inherent capability for learning.

The Inner Game approach (see "The Inner Game™") is about unlearning the personal and cultural habits that interfere with our ability to learn and perform. The goal is simple, if not easy: to give ourselves and our teams greater access to our innate abilities. The approach can be summarized in a simple formula:

Performance = Potential – Interference

"Potential" includes all of our capabilities—actualized or latent—as well as our ability to learn; "Interference" represents the ways that we undermine the fulfillment or expression of our own capacities.

Diminishing the Obstacles to Learning

We can achieve increased capacity for performance and learning either by actualizing potential or by decreasing interference—or by a combination of both. In my experience, the natural learning process—which is how we actualize potential—is gradual and ongoing. By contrast, reducing interference can have an immediate and far-reaching impact on learning and levels of performance. Thus, a successful model for skill development must take into account the phenomenon of interference.

But beware: The barriers to learning are often well guarded and may become even more entrenched when challenged. Coaches must generally be gentle in their approach to surfacing interference to learning and perfor-

THE INNER GAME™

Every game is composed of two parts: an *outer* game and an *inner* game. The outer game is played in an external arena to overcome external obstacles in the way of reaching external goals; the inner game focuses on internal obstacles as well as internal goals. The Inner Game is an approach to learning and coaching that brings the relatively neglected skills from the inner game to bear on success in the outer game. Its principles and methods were first articulated in the best-selling sports book, *The Inner Game of Tennis* (Random House, 1974), and were expanded upon in *Inner Tennis, Playing the Game* (1976); *Inner Skiing* (1976); and *The Inner Game of Golf* (1979). *The Inner Game of Work*, based on my work with major corporations interested in more effective ways to grow the capabilities of their people, is being published by Random House in 1998.

mance in an individual or team. Hints, suggestions, and indirect probing, though they may seem to take longer than a more direct approach, are usually more successful over the long run.

I learned a great deal about interference and how to help people work through it while coaching tennis and golf—two sports in which the obstacles to performance are difficult to disguise. And I have continued to find these sports excellent examples for exposing hidden obstacles to learning and performance. In addition, tennis and golf show the kinds of results that can occur when one succeeds in diminishing the impact of interference.

One of my favorite examples is what I call "the uh-oh experience." A tennis ball is coming toward a player who thinks she has a weak backhand. As the ball approaches, she thinks, "Here comes a probable mistake." She tightens her muscles, steps back defensively as if to avoid the threat, then slashes jerkily at the ball. When this action results in either an error or an easy shot for the opponent, she confirms to herself, "I really do have a terrible backhand," and unwittingly sets herself up for the same results on the next similar shot.

If a coach tried to correct each of the elements of the player's stroke that were incorrect, it would take months of "learning." However, if the coach worked at eliminating the player's negative self-talk by focusing her attention instead on perceiving the details of the ball's trajectory, most of the positive behavioral changes would take place without conscious effort.

Working at changing a player's perception instead of his or her behavior saves time and frustration for both student and coach.

Below is a partial list of obstacles to growing capability:

• **The assumption that "I already know."** Professionals often feel that they must present the appearance of already knowing everything and already being perfectly competent. This is an obstacle to learning that young children do not share.

• **The assumption that learning means remediation.** For many people, the suggestion that they should learn means there is something wrong with them or their level of performance.

• **Fear of being judged.** We learn this early, through teachers and parents who used judgment as a means to control behavior and effort.

• **Doubt.** The uncertainty we feel when we face the unknown is a prerequisite for learning. Young children are not embarrassed by not knowing something. However, as we age, we are taught to feel stupid or incompetent if we lack knowledge or experience or are unable to perform up to expectations. We are especially vulnerable to this feeling when faced with the challenge of unlearning something. The prospect of acknowledging that we might have invested time and effort in a perspective that is no longer valid can seem especially threatening.

• **Trying too hard to learn and to appear learned.** This phenomenon is a derivative of fear and doubt, and leads to constricted potential and mistakes. Our errors then confirm our self-doubt and bring about the very outcome that we feared.

Revealing the barriers to learning and performance can be an important first step in maximizing an individual's or a team's potential. To find the greatest leverage for reducing obstacles to learning in the workplace, I believe we should start with our definition of work itself. The way we see "work" has an impact on how we perceive everything we do in the workplace.

What Is Work?

If you ask executives the meaning of the word *work*, they focus on work as *doing* something—as accomplishing a goal, such as providing a product or service. In other words, to many people, work means performance. But definitions that equate work with performance can be limiting, especially in the current business environment.

Are there other results of work? When I ask executives this question, they generally offer responses that refer to two other distinct aspects of work. One is the domain of *experience*: How you feel while working is also a result of work. While working, people feel satisfaction, meaning, accomplishment, and challenge, as well as frustration, stress, anxiety, and boredom. Everyone at work experiences feelings that range from misery to fulfillment.

A second set of answers fall into the category of *learning*: While working, you can grow; develop know-how and skills; improve your ability to communicate, plan, strategize, and so on. Like performance and experience, learning is a universal and fundamentally human result of work—people of all ages, cultures, and levels of expertise are either learning and growing or stagnating and "devolving" while working. Adults can learn while working, just as children learn naturally while playing.

The Work Triangle

How are these fundamental results of work—performance, experience, and learning—related? They are unquestionably interdependent. If individuals aren't learning, their performance will decline over time; if their predominant experience of work is boredom or stress, both learning and performance will suffer. These three results can be represented in a mutually supportive "Work Triangle," with performance at the apex, and experience and learning at the base angles (see "The Work Triangle," p. 74).

When I ask a group of executives, "Which of the three work results gains the greatest support and encouragement in your work environment?" their response is overwhelmingly, "Performance." I then place my marking pen at the center of the Work Triangle and slowly draw a line toward the performance apex. "How much more priority is performance given over learning and enjoyment?" I ask. As the pen reaches the top of the triangle, a voice usually says, "Stop there." In response, the majority chants, "Keep going," until the line has gone past the apex and is several inches outside the tri-

THE WORK TRIANGLE

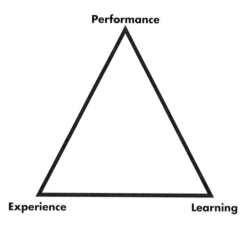

Performance

Experience   **Learning**

The fundamental results of work—performance, experience, and learning—are interdependent. If individuals aren't learning, their performance will decline over time; if their predominant experience of work is boredom or stress, both learning and performance will suffer.

angle. There is a general chuckle and a sense of a common understanding of corporate priorities.

In the competitive world of business, it is easy to see why performance may be given priority over learning and experience. But what are the consequences of pursuing performance at the expense of learning and experience? In any but the shortest time frame, the consequences are dire: Performance itself will fall. And what will be management's typical response? More pressure on performance, resulting in even less time and fewer resources directed toward learning or quality of experience.

How does the emphasis on performance play out in practice? Take your average sales manager who meets weekly with his sales representatives. The conversation usually focuses on performance issues, such as, How many calls did you make? What were the results of those calls in terms of sales? What are your plans for next week?

But what if the manager were committed to his own learning, as well as to his team's development? He might also ask: What did you find out from customers that you didn't know before—about their resistances, their needs, their perception of our products, how we compare to our competitors? How are different customers responding to our latest promotion? Did you gain any insights into your own selling skills? What is the competition doing? What are you interested in finding out next week? Did you learn anything that might help others on the team?

Our definition of work should include the worker's experience and learning, as well as his or her performance. The real value of this redefinition of work is that it includes me as an individual. I directly and immediately benefit from the learning and experience components of the Work Triangle. The "Experience" side of the triangle reminds me that I can't afford to neglect personal fulfillment during my working hours in the hope of enjoying myself only during vacation time or on weekends. I can never replace the hours of my life I spend at work, so I need to make the most of them.

The "Learning" side of the triangle reminds me that my future work prospects depend on the growth in my capabilities. Even if I'm fired from my present job, I take with me what I have learned, which I can leverage into productive and valued performance elsewhere. When my customers, managers, teammates, and the surrounding culture pressure me for performance results, the Work Triangle helps me remember that the person producing those results is important, too. I neglect my own learning and quality of experience at great peril to myself as well as to my future levels of performance.

The Tunnel Vision of Performance Momentum

The definition of work that focuses strictly on performance results at the expense of learning and experience produces a kind of tunnel vision that prevents workers from being fully aware and focused. I call this state of unconsciousness "performance momentum." At its worst, performance momentum is a series of actions an individual performs without true consciousness of how they relate to his or her most important priorities. Some call this mode of operation "fire-fighting." Examples include getting so caught up in a game of tennis that you forget it is a game, or engaging in conversations that undermine a relationship for the sake of merely winning an argument. In short, performance momentum means getting caught up in an action to the extent that you forget the purpose of the action.

I don't know of a more fundamental problem facing workers today. When individuals are caught up in performance momentum, they tend to forget not only important performance goals, but also their fundamental purpose as human beings. For example, my need to finish an article by the requested deadline obscures the reasons I chose to write the article in the first place, and dampens the natural enjoyment of expressing my thoughts and convictions. The person caught up in performance momentum neglects learning, growth, and the inherent quality of the work experience.

Learning is an increased capacity to perform; performance is the evidence that the capacity exists.

The tunnel vision that results from performance momentum is difficult to escape when individuals are working in a team that confirms and enforces the focus on performance. Any activity that is not seen as driving directly toward the goal is viewed as suspect. However, when a team or individual sacrifices the learning and experience sides of the Work Triangle to performance momentum, long-term performance suffers. More important, however, the individual suffers. And because the individual constitutes the building block of the team, the team suffers as well.

Balancing the Work Triangle

A simple method for assessing the balance among the three elements in the Work Triangle is to evaluate the way an individual or team articulates performance goals in comparison with learning and experience goals. It is revealing that many employees, when asked about learning or experience goals, are vague and express less conviction than when discussing performance goals. Setting clear learning goals is a good way to begin rebalancing the Work Triangle.

However, the distinction between learning and performance is often blurred. Even individuals who have worked on plans for the development of their competencies often fall into the trap of expressing their learning goals in terms of performance; for example, "I want to learn to focus more on the customer"; "I want to learn to reach higher sales quotas"; and "I'm working on learning how to get a promotion." The general rule for distinguishing between learning and performance goals is that learning can be viewed as a change that takes place *within* an individual, while performance takes place *on the outside*. Learning is an increased capacity to perform; performance is the evidence that the capacity exists.

A good way to focus on learning goals is through the acronym QUEST.

Q—**qualities** or attributes you might want to develop in yourself or others

U—increased **understanding** of the components of any person, situation, or system

E—development of **expertise**, knowledge, or skills

S—capacity for **strategic**, or **systemic**, thinking

T—capacity to optimize what you do with **time**

Teams and individuals can use QUEST to help form goals regarding what capabilities they want to develop. To be most effective, these objectives should support immediate performance goals but at the same time apply to many future performance challenges.

Coaching: A Conversation That Promotes Learning

When executives list the qualities, skills, and expertise they want from employees, they often list intangible attributes, such as creativity, accountability, sense of humor, team player, problem solver, and so on. So, how can you get the qualities and capabilities you want from people? The first response to this question is usually, "We have to do a better job in hiring." Clearly, it is important to hire capable people. But the real question is how to build the capabilities in the people you have hired, and how to keep those qualities from diminishing.

Unfortunately, the tools of managing performance are not particularly useful for promoting or developing important qualities and core skills. And it is difficult to imagine a course that teaches the rudiments of initiative or cooperation. So what is left? The word I use for the capacity to promote such desired attributes is *coaching*.

Coaching is a way of being, listening, asking, and speaking that draws out and augments characteristics and potential that are already present in a person. An effective coaching relationship creates a safe and challenging environment in which learning can take place. Coaches know that an oak tree already exists within an acorn. They have seen the one grow into the other, over time and under the right conditions, and are committed to providing those conditions to the best of their abilities. Successful coaches continually learn how best to "farm" the potential they are given to nurture.

A primary role of the coach is to stop performance momentum by calling a time out and providing questions or perspective that can encourage learning. Actual learning happens through experience—taking actions, observing the results, and modifying subsequent actions. To turn a work experience into a learning experience, a particular mindset must be established beforehand. Establishing this perspective can be done through something I call a "set-up conversation," which an individual can conduct alone through self-talk or with a coach. The set-up conversation helps make the learner aware of the possibilities that the imminent work experience could yield. In conducting one of these conversations, the coach asks questions that aid in focusing the individual's or team's attention.

At the end of a work experience, the coach and individual can hold a "debrief conversation." During this interchange, they might "mine" the gold of what was learned and refine questions to take into the next work experience. In this way, experience itself becomes the teacher. The coach's role becomes helping the learner ask valuable questions of the "teacher" and interpret the answers.

Coaching is very different from what we are generally taught as managers or teachers. We cannot teach work teams and individuals how to grow capabilities—in the sense of the transference of information in a classroom environment. Nor can we build capabilities through managerial techniques—for example, requiring certain abilities and rewarding employees when they display them or punishing them when they don't. Neither can we measure learning, because we can't directly observe it. In sum, it is the learner alone who controls the process and perceives its benefits. Managers don't even need to reward employees for learning—if learning indeed takes place, it will lead to improved performance. And employers generally award bonuses, raises, and promotions based on an increase in a worker's performance results.

Employees and managers cannot afford to wait for their corporate cultures to become learning cultures. Workers benefit from an expanded definition of work that includes learning and experience goals, and therefore must make the commitment to achieve those objectives. But companies also benefit from this new perspective on work. Wise are the corporate leaders who recognize that redefining work in this way is a difficult task, but that the company and its shareholders also gain advantages from a balanced Work Triangle. The best managers will provide what support and resources they can to the effort, and will make it their mission to shape their workplace into an optimal learning environment. The payoff will be improved business results and a corporate culture that attracts employees who equally value growth in capabilities. ⤶

Tim Gallwey is credited with founding the field of sports psychology. His four bestselling books on *The Inner Game* have deeply influenced the worlds of business and sports. For the last 15 years, Tim has spent most of his time working with companies that want to find a better way to implement change.

Chapter Seven

Creating a New Workplace: Making a Commitment to Community

by Greg Zlevor

—*"People listen to my ideas."*

—*"Within the first two weeks, everyone I worked with knew my name."*

—*"I'm more than a dishwasher. Who I am and what I think counts."*

These comments came from production workers at Rhino Foods, a specialty dessert producer in Vermont. Although I have worked with many companies, the spirit at Rhino struck me as unusually friendly, personal, and accepting. The workers felt that they were supported and valued, and the company culture exhibited a high level of trust and collaboration.

How did the people at Rhino Foods create such an atmosphere? What actually went on within and between people that fostered "healthy connection" or "community"? And how might this "community" have helped Rhino Foods become a learning organization?

In order to become a community of learners, we must be willing to inquire into our deepest assumptions. As we take those initial steps outside of our comfort zone and begin learning how to work and be together in new ways, we may find that building community is one of the most challenging aspects of the learning organization journey.

Many traditional, hierarchical organizations are struggling with long histories of distrust, detachment, and little companionship. Unfortunately, these patterns of alienation are a lot more common in organizations than patterns of community. Yet, even in organizations characterized by alienation, some pockets of healthy relationships and behavior endure. Consequently, community is not an all-or-nothing phenomenon. All groups, including Rhino Foods, exist somewhere along the continuum of "living in community"—and their placement on that continuum shifts continuously. Determining the location of your team or organization on that continuum is the first step in building a community of learners.

"Dis-ciety"

When people in a group feel secure, trusted, and connected, and consider themselves partners in creating a learning environment, that group can be characterized as having a high level of community. On the other hand, when people feel threatened, misled, and undervalued in a group, and act in ways that make others feel the same, the relationships are devoid of companionship or community. This far end of the continuum represents society at its worst—what I call a "disciety" (dis-society).

In a company that operates in disciety, individuals or teams may exaggerate budget requests to get more resources, or lie about their results, skills, or abilities in order to look good. A common sentiment is, "I have to be political in order to survive." Employees spend a great deal of time and energy determining which side they need to be on, who their allies are, and how they can best protect themselves. The goal is not to pursue what is most beneficial for the team or company, but how to look impressive or get ahead.

Because of the huge energy drain this creates, people do not push themselves unless they see the potential for personal gain; they do the minimum just to get by. Over time, dysfunctional relationships between individuals and departments develop. These differences can lead to conflict and tension, and it becomes more important to make a good point than to listen and understand. As a result, meetings resemble a battlefield where more energy is spent pulling and tugging than reflecting or comprehending.

Qualities of Community

In contrast, a community such as the one at Rhino Foods can bring out the best in people. Such a community is characterized by mutual service, encouragement, and support. It is based, first and foremost, on authentic communication—a natural, truthful, and honest revealing of one person to another in an open and accepting relationship (see "Community-Building Dynamics," p. 84). Because people feel safe, they can feel comfortable expressing their concerns, desires, expectations, and accomplishments, even if they fall short of personal or company expectations.

For example, in the midst of a dilemma at Rhino Roods, founder and CEO Ted Castle employed the values of community to work collectively on a solution. An anticipated drop in orders had led to production overcapacity. Rather than lay off workers, he chose to disclose the problem to all of the employees at a company meeting.

At this meeting, Ted asked for a task force to develop solutions consistent with the company's stated vision: "Rhino Foods is a company whose actions are inspired by the spirit of discovery, innovation, and creativity. Our purpose is to impact the manner in which business is done." He allowed the group significant autonomy, which increased their security and encouraged them to be honest and vulnerable.

The result was a unique alternative: Instead of downsizing, Rhino Foods initiated an exchange program in which certain Rhino employees would temporarily go to work for other companies. This enabled the partner companies to fill their personnel needs with skilled workers on a short-term basis, while Rhino workers continued to receive paychecks. This creative solution allowed Rhino to maintain internal morale and avoid significant financial losses.

Community Spectrum

No group is ever continually in community. The continuum between community and disciety depicts the different stages people experience when moving in and out of community (see "Community/Disciety Continuum," p. 85). In order to enhance learning in organizations, it is important to work toward fostering an environment that is consistently closer to the "community" end of the continuum.

COMMUNITY-BUILDING DYNAMICS

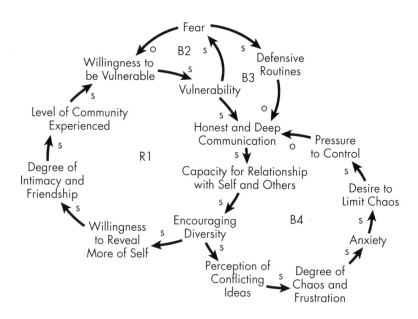

The reinforcing process of community-building begins with individuals' willingness to be vulnerable. Becoming more vulnerable opens up honest and deep communication, which expands one's capacity for relationship with self and others and encourages greater diversity. With increased diversity comes a greater willingness to reveal more of one's self, which deepens intimacy and heightens the experience of community, further reinforcing people's ability to be vulnerable (R1).

There are, however, balancing forces that can thwart community-building efforts and kick the reinforcing process in reverse. Increasing one's vulnerability can lead to heightened fear, which can decrease one's willingness to be vulnerable (B2), and/or the fear can trigger defensive routines that shut down honest communication (B3). In addition, increased diversity can lead to conflict and increased frustration, followed by a desire to limit chaos and to control—all of which counter efforts for honest and deep communication (B4).

There are three stages of development between Disciety and Community—Dysfunctional, Functional, and Formative. The Dysfunctional stage is the one closest to Disciety, and is characterized by poli-

COMMUNITY/DISCIETY CONTINUUM

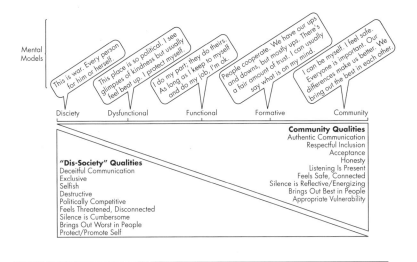

Mental Models

This is war. Every person for him or herself.

This place is so political. I see glimpses of kindness but usually feel beat up. I protect myself.

I do my part; they do theirs. As long as I keep to myself and do my job, I'm ok.

People cooperate. We have our ups and downs, but mostly ups. There's a fair amount of trust. I can usually say what is on my mind.

I can be myself. I feel safe. Everyone is important. Our differences make us better. We bring out the best in each other.

| Disciety | Dysfunctional | Functional | Formative | Community |

"Dis-Society" Qualities
Deceitful Communication
Exclusive
Selfish
Destructive
Politically Competitive
Feels Threatened, Disconnected
Silence is Cumbersome
Brings Out Worst in People
Protect/Promote Self

Community Qualities
Authentic Communication
Respectful Inclusion
Acceptance
Honesty
Listening Is Present
Feels Safe, Connected
Silence is Reflective/Energizing
Brings Out Best in People
Appropriate Vulnerability

tics and pain. In the Functional stage, people are basically left alone as long as they do their job. The Formative stage, however, is where people begin to cooperate and share their personal thoughts. Finally, Community is a place of safety in which diverse views and individuals are accepted.

In order to move a group toward community, individuals need to begin or further their practice of the disciplines of community (see Community Qualities in "Community/Disciety Continuum," above). Practicing these disciplines can help move a company's culture from one place on the continuum to the next. For example, "Listening Is Present" may mean that the person in charge of a meeting provides time for workers to share whatever is on their mind. "Respectful Inclusion" might mean that a manager shares information received from superiors, or includes constituents in the decision-making process. Each of these disciplines of community has an opposite quality that promotes disciety; the challenge is to recognize which qualities are being expressed at any one time and purposefully work toward developing those that enhance community.

Whatever your current reality, living the journey of community building is more natural and important than attempting to preserve a specific condition. Over time, as a group practices the disciplines of healthy relationships, it may one day find itself "in" community, a space characterized by support and safety. This is a peak experience occasionally felt during the process. Like any feeling, however, it continually changes. Therefore, a mature group may bask in, but never cling to, the feeling of being "in" community. Instead, it learns to continue practicing the disciplines of healthy relationships while accepting its present condition.

Where Do You Want to Be?

Where is your company on the community continuum? Where do you want to be? There are three factors to consider in determining a group's placement on the community continuum: condition, intention, and action. These factors represent a group's current reality, its vision, and what it is doing to close the gap. To determine a group's *condition*, we need to survey the group's experience of safety, authenticity, connectedness, and respect. The greater the number of individuals who are experiencing these characteristics, the healthier the relationships. Second, *intention* reveals what a group wants or desires. Questions that surface a group's intentions include, "Do we want to overcome our disagreements?" and "Are we willing to be honest and work to resolve this issue?" The group's *actions* determine its present ability. By observing communication patterns such as behavior at meetings, etc., it is possible to see what a group is currently able to do and where it needs to work more.

For example, after someone makes a suggestion or offers a new idea in a meeting, do you hear, "Yeah, but . . . " or "Maybe, but I think . . . " or "I disagree. I believe . . . "? If so, the group members may need to practice suspending judgments in order to improve their listening. On the other hand, if you hear "Why do you suggest that?" or "Say more about your idea," and members take the time to respectfully listen and understand one another, then deeper and more authentic communication is being practiced.

It is critical to remember, however, that actions alone do not reveal a group's direction or condition. Community is not determined by the presence or absence of pain or conflict, but by a group's ability to deal with those issues. A group of people who are experiencing conflict or pain may appear to be moving toward disciety, but if their overall intent is one of care, con-cern, and commitment, this experience is a likely step toward community. On the other hand, people in a similar situation who are working toward individual gain at the expense of the whole are probably moving toward disciety. Consequently, both intention and action are critical determinants.

Community in a Learning Organization

The process of developing a learning community touches upon all of the disciplines of a learning organization. For example, a shared vision provides the purpose, coherence, and energy for the organization. But in order to uncover what visions matter to people, the people themselves need to mat-ter. Therefore, a genuine respect and concern for personal visions is one of the building blocks for a shared vision.

The process of building a learning organization also promotes continual examination, reflection, learning, and growth. It strives to uncover limiting behaviors and attitudes, while developing a deeper awareness of the struc-tures and events that foster them. In order to receive honest input and per-sonal commitment from employees, a relative level of security must exist. When people feel comfortable, it is easier for them to risk "not knowing" and therefore to open themselves to learning.

For example, Rhino Foods stimulated input and deepened trust by sched-uling "listening" sessions before each production shift begins. This session allowed all personnel to voice concerns and hopes for the upcoming day. The position of listening session leader rotated among all experienced work-ers; because of the rotating leadership, a degree of trust had been built over time.

Rhino Foods also recognized that community is an important factor for nourishing "personal mastery" or personal growth. Rhino encouraged employees to increase their personal mastery through its WANTS program, in which Rhino employees' facilitated other employees achievement of per-sonal goals. The goals do not need to deal with improving Rhino—and the specific wants an employee works on with his or her facilitator, on company time, is confidential and up to the employee. The employees who facilitated this process with others were trained by the company. Marlene Dailey,

---

PITFALLS, ILLUSIONS, AND
STUMBLING BLOCKS ON THE ROAD TO COMMUNITY

Before we embark on the process of building community, it is important to be aware of the potential dangers. The path toward building authentic learning communities is dotted with land mines and stumbling blocks. Many of them are merely myths that we must challenge if we are to achieve true community:

Myth #1: "If we build community, money will follow." Not so. It is possible to do all the right things, live with integrity, and not necessarily make more money. Community and profitability are not synonymous—but employees who find greater meaning and purpose, develop better communication, and work more easily together will naturally be drawn to organizations with a high level of commitment to community. Organizations with employees committed to a common vision, teamwork, and honest communication are an enviable resource. This resource often improves the health and profits of an organization over the long term.

Myth #2: "Community and hierarchy are incompatible." An organization with leaders who are willing to listen, respect, and serve employees can go further in creating community than a group of equals who are unwilling, unable, or both. The presence and practice of community-building disciplines is thus more critical than the presence or absence of hierarchy.

Myth #3: "Building community is the responsibility of top management." The idea of building community may start at the top, but how far it spreads depends on the drive and commitment of people at all levels. If management "railroads" the community initiative through the organization, it is doomed to fail. The more mutual the endeavor, the better the results.

Myth #4: "A community building *program* will create community." Programs or initiatives do not create community—people's desires and actions do. Developing healthier relationships takes time, energy, and commitment. It is better to start small and build momentum than to create high expectations and be disillusioned.

---

director of Human Resources, pointed to the WANTS program as a contributing factor in the company's high morale and low employee turnover.

Knowledge and Commitment to Community

To *know about* community and to know community are quite different. The first implies that building a community is simply about learning a few concepts, designing a series of trainings, and charting the impact on performance to determine whether the initiative is successful. The latter, to "know" community, requires being personally committed to and involved in a deeper and more profound process.

Knowing community means committing your whole self to a way of interacting with people that promotes respect, tolerance, and growth; to a process of living that begins but never ends; and to relationships that go deeper than simple appearances.

Community is thus both a process (directed by intention and action) and a place (a particular condition). The more people work at being together in the process, the better they become at being a community. Ultimately, community is both a way of being and a place to be—a journey and a destination.   ⤸

Greg Zlevor is president of Westwood International, a consulting company specializing in organizational and teamwork strategies for business and groups. He is also the founder of the *Community in Organizations Conference,* an annual event that investigates creative relationships within organizations.

The "Community Building Dynamics" diagram was developed with assistance from Stephanie Ryan and Craig Fleck.

Building a Core Competence in Community

by Kazimierz Gozdz

I recently worked with a group in a high-tech computer company that once had a very alive sense of community. The people felt connected, efficient, and there was a high sense of trust within the group. Productivity and learning were phenomenal.

Results were so good, in fact, that management infused the group with millions of dollars to upgrade its working environment and add more staff. But a year later, this group no longer felt like a community, and everyone was afraid to say so. Management pretended that everything was as it had been, and anyone who offered evidence to the contrary was considered a traitor.

In examining the history of this group's process, it was easy to see that no one had expended effort to keep alive the one resource that had made the group so successful: its spirit of community. Everyone just assumed that if management financed an expansion of the project, the sense of community would automatically continue.

A collective spirit of community, such as the one experienced by the original group, is highly prized. Yet more often than not, actions intended to preserve this spirit drive it out instead. In the case of the computer firm, the development of community was largely ignored to death.

What Is a Community?

A mature community is characterized by an inclusiveness of diverse people and information, semipermeable boundaries, and a systems-oriented paradigm. In such a workplace, there is an openness to creativity and innovation. The organization becomes, in effect, a group of leaders who embody a profound sense of mutual respect and have the ability to fight gracefully while transcending differences. The benefits of corporate community include a profound sense of trust and collaboration, which leads to a coherent organizational vision.

A collective spirit of community, such as the one experienced by the original group, is highly prized. Yet more often than not, actions intended to preserve this spirit drive it out instead.

How can an organization consciously and strategically develop competence in community building? It must first make the commitment to learn and grow as a community throughout its life cycle. Developing such a competence depends on a balanced growth of three interrelated elements: the experience of interconnectedness; sustainable collective intelligence; and learning architecture (see "Core Competence in Community Building"). Sustaining community over the long term also requires an organization to go through several stages of growth, each with its own set of developmental challenges. By anticipating these challenges, we can prepare to respond in ways that optimize growth and change while minimizing chaos.

Interconnectedness

Almost anyone who has survived a significant crisis in a group knows the spirit of community. Starting a new organization, enduring a tragedy such as the death of a colleague or friend, or experiencing a natural disaster can all lead to a spirit of interconnectedness in a group. In these cases, community arises as the result of a group's need for survival.

CORE COMPETENCE IN COMMUNITY BUILDING

Developing a competency in community building depends on a balanced growth of three interrelated elements: the experience of interconnectedness, sustainable collective intelligence, and learning architecture. Together they form a system that we call a "core competence" in sustainable community.

In business, this survival goal can be the starting point for developing a culture that deliberately fosters community throughout the course of the workday. Rather than depending on haphazard events such as crises, a team can actively nurture its capability to create experiences of interconnectedness through authentic communication. Paradoxically, it does this by acknowledging differences.

The typical organization is essentially what M. Scott Peck, author of *The Different Drum: Community Making and Peace*, calls a "pseudo-community," an organization unwilling or unable to acknowledge its differences. However, a group can be taught the discipline of learning to acknowledge and transcend these differences. If members are willing to learn how to face reality together, they can develop authentic and vulnerable communication. Through such a process, the organization can become aware of its barriers to true community.

When teams and organizations manage to experience interconnectedness—with its benefits of authentic communication, safety, and intimacy—they are often so enthusiastic about these benefits that they try to stay in this state continually. But after a while they notice that their attempts actually create less sense of community. The lesson here is that the spirit of interconnectedness in a community is not a permanent state. It ebbs and flows with the community's life cycle—and when it is not present, it may be a signal that one or both of the other two aspects of core competence require attention.

Sustainable Collective Intelligence

A second aspect of developing a community has do with enhancing the collective intelligence of a group. If a group cannot convert collective intelligence into organizational action, it can easily become a support group rather than a high-performing learning community. Creating such collective intelligence means actively nurturing the sense of community while simultaneously acting and making decisions that can improve the group's thinking skills.

One method for developing collective intelligence is the dialogue process introduced by physicist David Bohm. Dialogue focuses on creating shared meaning by surfacing and examining assumptions within a group. It emphasizes the importance of rational and cognitive group learning. As David Bohm described it, "[the word 'dialogue'] suggests a stream of meaning flowing among and through us and between us. This will make possible a flow of meaning in the whole group, out of which will come some new understanding."

In business, this survival goal can be the starting point for developing a culture that deliberately fosters community throughout the course of the workday.

Dialogue is very effective for exploring fundamental assumptions underlying group thought, but because of its focus on cognition, it limits the range of emotion within a group. An alternative is to incorporate Bohm's cognitive emphasis with Peck's focus on authentic feeling states and stages of community building (see "Community Building: A Four-Stage Model").

COMMUNITY BUILDING: A FOUR-STAGE MODEL

Building or experiencing community can be described as a four-stage process:

Pseudo-community. During this stage the group pretends that it already is a community and that differences do not exist. The decision-making process and the nature of relationships go unchallenged, and "politically correct" or polite behavior dominates.

Chaos. The sense of apparent control and order is disrupted when differences emerge. The group tries to obliterate these individual differences by polarizing topics, looking for winners and losers, or changing each other. Replication and duplication of what has worked in the past is mandated, and decisions are made via competition, political power, and authoritarian control.

Emptiness. Having failed to control or organize its way into community, the group steps into true chaos; uncertainty and ambiguity replace control. The group begins the work of self-examination, giving up personal obstacles, barriers, and agendas. It is the beginning of true listening, where the group's decision-making process becomes collaborative.

Community. Having emptied itself of its previous mental models, the group is available for authentic communication. Authentic connection is achieved by acknowledging differences. In this safe place, creativity emerges. The group as a whole makes decisions co-creatively, learns as an entity, and innovates as a whole.

Combining dialogue and community building can allow a group to shift rapidly between "head" and "heart," allowing for a collective intelligence that can be sustained more easily over time.

Learning Architecture

Collective thought and action are required in order for groups to change the complex architecture that either supports or inhibits community. The learning architecture of community consists primarily of the systems and structures that sustain memory and learning in the organization over time. The compensation system, career development process, style of leadership, methods for distribution of power and governance, and physical structure of the site all affect a group's ability to experience itself as an authentic community.

Understanding how the organization's learning architecture enhances or blocks community is critical to realizing the trust, joy, and flexibility of community. No amount of attention to team spirit or learning will be productive if the structures of the organization cannot or will not be changed to support community. More often than not, an organization that is having difficulty sustaining a sense of community is operating with systems that create fragmentation or disempowerment.

Systems thinking's emphasis on structural diagramming and identifying high-leverage interventions can help in creating structures that support community. This work is critical, because even when the organization's leadership politically backs the enhancement of community, if the organizational structures are prohibitive they can inadvertently destroy hope.

Sustaining Community

With the actualization of the three aspects of core competence—interconnectedness, sustainable collective intelligence, and learning architecture—an organization takes its first steps to becoming a community. Developing a core competence in these three aspects, however, is just the starting point for long-term growth. Like a child that grows to maturity, all three elements must grow in harmony and balance for long-term health and vitality. And just as humans go through infancy, adolescence, and adulthood, communities go through necessary growth stages and transitions as they mature (see "Community: Stages of Maturation").

By definition, growth necessitates a certain amount of pain. If the organizational community avoids the pain of growth, it stops the learning process. But if it consciously embraces the three developmental learning challenges described below, an organization will find opportunities to grow spiritually, psychologically, and competitively.

Paradigm Shift—Embracing Wholeness

The first developmental stage in sustaining community is to wrestle with the assumptions of our prevailing mechanistic paradigm. Businesses cannot sustain themselves as communities or learning organizations unless they become capable of embracing a paradigm of wholeness.

COMMUNITY: STAGES OF MATURATION

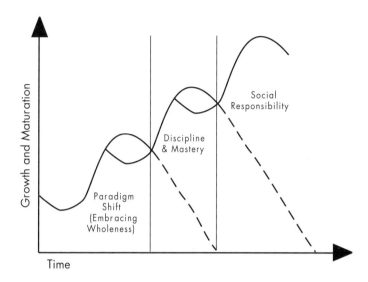

The curves represent critical transitions of growth and decline associated with the three stages of a community's maturation. If any stage is ignored or missed, it invariably leads to a decline in the community (depicted by the dotted lines). Such communities revert to pseudo-community, growing only in age, not in problem-solving capability or wisdom.

Although a community-based perspective can be temporarily grafted onto an organizational world view that seeks answers in linear causality, such a transplant will not "take." Community responds best to cyclical, nonlinear processes. Organizations destroy community when they treat it like a mechanical process made up of linear cause-and-effect relationships.

In his groundbreaking work on paradigms, Thomas Kuhn explained that a group holding onto old ideas and values will often choose to die conserving them rather than risk the learning required for change. The only remedy to this situation that Kuhn offered was to wait for people to die off over time, thus paving the way for a new paradigm to emerge. Unlike the ill-fated groups that Kuhn described, businesses can use the technology of community building to make the transition between paradigms consciously.

A typical organization that has been successful and profitable for extended periods of time can fall out of touch with the "real world," and the company's culture can become unquestioned, much like a paradigm. When this happens, the leadership of the organization needs to pierce this unreality by challenging mental models and fostering an environment of trust where a new worldview can actually take hold.

However, since our traditional organizations create and legitimize paradigms, acts of individual leadership are usually ineffective in changing them. The community-building process must therefore challenge and transform the collective worldview. At this stage in the community's life, the principle leverage point for growth resides in creating effective ways for the collective intelligence of the group to create new individual and organizational models of reality.

Discipline and Mastery

No organization can have a positive learning environment or feel like a "family" at all times. The evolution of a living community includes turbulent times that occur as we encounter one another's and the organization's underdeveloped areas. A learning organization that embraces community as a core competence thus requires day-in and day-out practice of what I call "discipline and mastery," so that the community and the individuals within it move toward optimum competency and aligned organizational purpose.

M. Scott Peck and Peter Senge both see learning as a lifelong program of study—what they call a "discipline." In *The Fifth Discipline*, Peter Senge explained, "By 'discipline' I do not mean 'enforced order' or 'means of punishment' but a body of theory and technique that must be put into practice. A discipline is a developmental path for acquiring certain skills or competencies. As with any discipline . . . anyone can develop proficiency through practice."

I believe that developing a core competence in community building requires four main leadership skills (originally described by Peck as a system of discipline):

• *Delay gratification.* Foster the ability to hold tension between the vision and the current reality, and be able to see the actual reality of a situation without jumping to problem solving. Embrace larger and more systemic views, avoiding the simplicity of linear causes and obvious solutions.

• *Dedication to the truth.* Boldly acknowledge what learning the organization needs to pursue. Seek to embrace unpleasant truths. Acknowledge the gap between intended and actual outcomes in order to remove the barriers to learning.

• *Assume responsibility.* Practice willingness to act as a fearless learner, to move beyond blame or judgment of oneself or others for the purpose of learning. Take responsibility for change.

• *Balance learning.* Discipline must be subject to a system of checks and balances or it can easily lead to burnout, excessive work, or a "task master" mentality. To truly benefit from learning, we need to provide periods of "slack time" for integration, relaxation, and play. Without balance, learning is less effective—and no amount of discipline can substitute for compassion and care.

Social Responsibility

Once a learning organization has embraced a paradigm of wholeness and established itself as a sustainable learning community, it will find itself called to address its responsibility to the larger society. This final developmental stage is really just a starting place for another level of growth.

No amount of attention to team spirit or learning will be productive if the structures of the organization cannot or will not be changed to support community.

An organization at this level of development will discover that its impediments to community are intrinsically tied to the limitations and systems that govern the larger society. For example, in the West, interlocking systems of oppression (such as racism, sexism, and classism) will inevitably emerge as obstacles to sustaining the community. These larger social issues will have to be addressed within the organizational goals of the company. Many organizations are surprised by the level of tension and struggle that is intrinsic to a mature community. They expect that mature communities are tranquil. But community is paradoxical: the more spiritually mature it becomes, the deeper the concerns it struggles with.

The fully mature community will encounter turbulent times, because once individuals and organizations reach this level of social awareness, the organization will need to reclarify its fundamental vision, values, and purpose. It will require this new clarity to balance its vision against its need to act on social issues. Because of past experiences of interconnectedness, a community will undoubtedly recognize that its survival is linked to that of the larger society. It can then develop a social vision that complements the organization's profit-centered vision.

The Journey Toward Authenticity

In an effort to build sustainable communities, managers sometimes try to apply traditional management methods, much to the community's detriment. There is a difference, however, between the responsible measurement of results and measurement that kills incentive. Those managers who are preoccupied with measurement over results tend to ask: How is community defined? How can we measure it? What results has it produced so far? This kind of leadership leaves organizations starving for authentic connection, since individuals who are preoccupied with evaluation often do not have energy for the work of building community.

A business seeking to become a learning organization by developing a core competence in community is embarking upon a complex and rewarding journey. This journey includes making a shift from hiding complex problems to not only confronting them but actually using them to gain competitive advantage.

Embracing this journey provides a way for a business locked into an old paradigm, or stuck in the stage of pseudo-community, to transform itself into a more authentic community. Once learning and authentic connection become integrated, the organization can then release the talents and gifts of the community members in a way that produces results far beyond the capability of any one individual. ⌒

Kazimierz Gozdz is a partner in the Corporate Civility Group and a consulting member of the Society for Organizational Learning. Kaz has worked to build theory, practice, and methods for transforming organizations into thriving learning communities. He writes, speaks, and consults in the area of workplace community, serving as editor for *Community Building: Renewing Spirit and Learning in Business* (New Leaders Press, 1995) and as coauthor, with Peter M. Senge and Joseph Jaworski, of *Setting the Field: Creating the Conditions for Profound Institutional Change* (Society for Organizational Learning working paper).

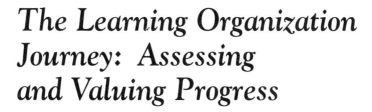

Chapter Nine

The Learning Organization Journey: Assessing and Valuing Progress

by Nils H. Bohlin and Paul Brenner

Suppose you have just been appointed the CKO—Chief Knowledge Officer—of your organization. You are responsible for managing the company's knowledge capital, including how it is created, maintained, and used. You understand the principles of organizational learning and agree that effective learning is the pathway to accelerated performance improvement. Now you need to determine the right approach for your organization, and how to get started.

It might help to think of organizational learning as an ongoing journey (see "Organizational Learning Journey: A Roadmap," p. 104). Although each company's path will look slightly different, assessing your organization's knowledge base and learning skills is a good place to start. This information provides a baseline against which you can measure your progress toward becoming a learning organization.

Learning Serves the Business Vision

Planning your organizational learning journey begins with knowing where you want to go. Articulating a vision for both the business and the organization will help define your destination—the higher purposes you want to serve through the specific learning initiatives. Starting with an organiza-

ORGANIZATIONAL LEARNING JOURNEY: A ROADMAP

Business vision	Learning needs	Knowledge base	Learning strategies
Organization vision		Learning practices	
		Learning climate	

Measure Progress and Reassess

The stages of the organizational learning journey include an articulation of the business and organizational vision, an evaluation of the company's learning needs, and the development of a learning strategy that will achieve the firm's learning objectives.

tional vision ensures that the learning needs of the company are driven by business and organization goals.

Different learning needs call for different learning styles and practices. For example, at Electricité de France, safety concerns do not allow nuclear power plant operators to experiment or to take risks on the job, so their learning takes the form of incremental improvements based on TQM techniques. By contrast, Kodak has experimented with electronic imaging products that go well beyond its traditional lines of chemical-based films—a change that may require the firm to learn how to redesign key processes. Because of this need, Kodak fosters a creative and relatively high-risk environment aimed at rethinking its business over the long term. Although they differ in style, the learning practices at each company match its particular learning needs.

Once you have articulated your company's business vision and defined its learning needs, you will want to get a better sense of the organization's current learning condition. To assess this, there are three key areas to consider:

• **Knowledge Base:** the strengths and weaknesses of your organization's knowledge base and the knowledge areas to be reinforced

- **Learning Practices:** the management and operating practices that foster or hinder learning
- **Learning Climate:** the work culture and its effect on learning.

Knowledge Base

In today's economy, knowledge, not capital assets, is the primary source of wealth. While there are some exciting new methods for measuring and valuing knowledge capital, few organizations have studied how they themselves create, store, and use that capital. You can start your learning assessment by mapping your organization's business processes in terms of knowledge generated and used.

This is exactly what one European company did recently. The company faced increasing pressures from global competitors in the baby-diaper business, as a recent result of product innovations. Company personnel began a knowledge base assessment by defining what the company knew how to do in all its business processes, and then assessed their knowledge position versus what they viewed as world-class practices. Then they unbundled the knowledge base into precisely defined areas of know-how, determined the competitive impact of each area, rated their own performance versus that of the competition, identified gaps in the knowledge base, and designed corrective actions (see "Strategic Knowledge Map," p. 106).

The results prompted a wake-up call. Company employees recognized that they needed to reinforce the company's knowledge base. They defined the areas of collaboration needed to fill the gaps in the base and entered several strategic alliances with other firms. The collaborative partners found the approach so helpful that they, in turn, initiated Strategic Knowledge Mapping in their own companies.

When you assess your firm's knowledge base, it's important to remember that knowledge comes in many forms, not just in databases and procedure manuals. Tacit knowledge—based on experience and practice—can be as important as explicit knowledge. For example, Matsushita developed a bread-making machine in the late 1980s. When early prototypes could not replicate the art of high-quality bread-making, developers apprenticed themselves to master breadmakers to discover the tacit knowledge that

STRATEGIC KNOWLEDGE MAP

Define the business context	Define the knowledge base in strategic terms	Draw implications and shape actions
• Summarize existing strategies within the industry • Identify success factors • Identify business processes	• Unbundle major business processes into specific areas of know-how • Classify know-how as base, key, pacing, or emerging • Assess your knowledge competitive position and define gaps	• Summarize knowledge in terms of strengths, weaknesses, opportunities, and threats • Define the knowledge areas for reinforcement actions • Define the knowledge reinforcement plan

The Strategic Knowledge Map provides a systematic way for a company to examine its knowledge base by defining its areas of know-how, determining the competitive impact of each area, rating its performance versus the competition, identifying gaps in the knowledge base, and designing correct actions.

these experts could not communicate explicitly. Your knowledge map should show the strategic importance of both tacit and explicit knowledge.

Learning Practices

Successful learning does not happen by accident. One hallmark of a learning organization is a purposeful learning approach designed to create knowledge and translate it into effective action. How can you create learning practices?

You can begin by looking for learning cycles. Successful learning typically follows a sequence:

1. *Shared awareness* of a need for learning;
2. A *common understanding* of the situation;
3. *Aligned actions*, with measured results;
4. *Joint review* and communication of results; and
5. *Collective reflection* about the learning process.

(For examples of these steps in action, see "Supporting the Learning Cycle" on p. 110–111.)

A summary way to view your company's existing learning practices is to compile an inventory of your organization's use of specific learning practices. This profile will provide a sense of where the organization perceives gaps between current conditions and the desired future reality, and can indicate priority areas for attention.

Learning Climate

In order to foster organizational learning, you should focus on enhancing individual and group skills, designing support structures for ongoing learning, and creating an overall organizational attitude that encourages learning. All of these aspects make up an organization's "learning climate."

A learning climate has both "soft" and "hard" components. On the soft side, cultural norms can either support or hinder learning. The hard side of a learning climate includes the structures and technologies that support open communication, knowledge management, and teamwork. One way to sense your organization's learning climate is to look for evidence of the following conditions:

Curiosity. A culture that values curiosity and inquiry adopts learning behaviors naturally. Simulations and experiments follow from "what if" questions. Questions about what customers think and what competitors are doing lead to environmental scanning and targeted studies of the outside world.

For example, Sharp defines its product development vision as "optoelectronics," a grand but undefined term. The breadth and open-endedness of the term spurs the curiosity of employees, who ask, "What does that mean? How can this term fit my work?" The creation of Sharp's overhead projection computer display is one result of the creative tension prompted by such purposeful ambiguity.

Recognition of Conflict and Errors. Learning requires openness to new ideas, even when they generate controversy. Conflict should be welcomed as the means to develop common understanding, rather than suppressed for the sake of harmony.

Organizations that celebrate the discovery of errors, rather than search for blame, will learn from their mistakes. A good example of this comes from a team that writes documentation for electronics products. Each month the team celebrates the discovery of documentation errors with a bonfire of obsolete manuals—the bigger the better!

Leadership. The leader of a learning organization is not the traditional hero, individually responsible for tough decisions. Instead, he or she is the designer of corporate culture who accepts the uncertainty implied by experimentation. This is a very different model of leadership, and if it is embraced by top management, it is likely to be diffused to all management levels. Those being led can tell you which model of leadership is prevalent in your firm.

Staff Development. The implicit employment contract between a firm and its employees has changed. Long-term employment guarantees are being replaced by employer-supplied opportunities to maintain and expand knowledge and skills. Look for learning opportunities not just in the training department, but in job experiences that broaden responsibilities across functions.

Information and Communication Systems. Technological solutions to the challenges of creating, storing, and sharing knowledge include groupware, corporate knowledge bases, and videoconferencing. As you trace the flow of knowledge through your organization, look for how well these tech·nologies are used.

Team-Based Work. Some work environments encourage learning efforts by single individuals, while others foster collective work. Learning organizations tend to encourage interaction and problem solving by teams. To assess whether your organization values individuals or teams, look at the recognition and reward systems. Is performance measured individually or in groups? Do rewards go to stars or to stellar team efforts? Are major initiatives personalized (as when a project takes on the name of its leader, such as the Grace Commission) or do they remain the responsibility of teams?

Some artifacts are subtle. For example, when we visited the offices of a construction equipment producer, a manager explained that coffee stations were placed in such a way that the design staff and customer service staff were forced to share stations. This set-up guarantees that design staff have at least informal opportunities to learn from the voice of the customer.

INCOMPLETE LEARNING CYCLES

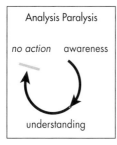

One way to diagnose learning problems is to look for patterns of learning cycles that are consistently broken. These three common examples show how learning processes can become derailed.

Incomplete Learning Cycles. Your search for learning practices should include problems as well as successes. One way to diagnose learning problems is to look for patterns of consistently broken learning cycles (see "Incomplete Learning Cycles," above). If your organization has many stories of fact-finding and analysis, but few examples of taking action, it may be trying to learn vicariously ("analysis paralysis"). If there is lots of action but little analysis and planning, your learning may be accidental at best (the "ready, fire, aim" approach). If your firm regularly progresses to aligned action but can't seem to learn from results, you may not have adequate measurement, review, and feedback systems in place. You "reinvent wheels" because the results from past wheel designs were never internalized.

Guidelines for Assessing Learning

Once you know what to look for as you assess your company's learning efforts—knowledge management processes, learning practices, and the learning climate—you need to know how to find them. The following activities can provide guidelines for assessing your company's progress:

Self-Assessment. Because learning is embedded in day-to-day activities and organizational culture, guided self-assessment can yield valid results. Train a member of each group in the principles of organizational learning

SUPPORTING THE LEARNING CYCLE

The following examples for each of the stage of the learning cycle may help you identify learning practices in your organization.

Generating Shared Awareness involves continuously assimilating internal and external information about problems and opportunities.

• Dell Computer holds regular Customer Advocate Meetings to share what support people have heard from customers with colleagues in product development, sales, and marketing.

• NUMMI rotates shop-floor employees through the plant to build shared awareness of new processes.

Creating Common Understanding requires tools and processes for creating a common understanding of key problems and opportunities and openly discussing options for action.

• Ford uses management simulators to experience the results of decisions without "betting the company."

• Royal Dutch/Shell has a rich history of using scenarios of possible oil industry trends as team-based planning exercises designed to develop a common approach to strategy.

• Du Pont maintains and publishes a reference model of all business processes.

Producing Aligned Action. The purpose of learning is to enable the organization to take more effective action. Alignment refers to the match between an organization's goals and its actions, and to the choreography of actions across divisions and over time.

• Honda helps to ensure that customer management and engineering actions are aligned by including representatives from sales, engineering, and product development in every project team.

Performing Joint Review. It is helpful to review and measure the results of actions in an open forum. The purpose is not to assign blame or praise, but to gain insight from the complete cycle and kick off the next cycle of performance improvement.

• Procordia, a Scandinavian consumer goods and healthcare group, undertook two major acquisitions simultaneously in 1990. In order to manage the integration of the two groups, it created a merger process organization

(*continued on next page*)

SUPPORTNG THE LEARNING CYCLE, *continued*

that masterminded and reviewed actions. Every second Friday during the four-month process, there was an all-afternoon meeting with the top management group to report on progress from the merger task forces.

Conducting Collective Reflection. In order to be purposeful about learning, it is important to reflect continuously on past and present operations and seek improvements in learning activities.

• British Petroleum uses a five-person unit reporting to the board of directors to derive lessons learned from past major projects.

• Boeing commissioned a group called Project Homework to dissect its past product development processes, leading to the successful development of the B757.

• L.L. Bean has a team devoted to improving its business process improvement process.

---

and have these people lead structured interviews that identify learning practices and climate factors. This training also prepares selected process members to facilitate the learning action plan that should follow an assessment.

Group Interviews. Interviews that are intended to tease out learning practices are better done in groups rather than one-on-one. This is because learning practices at the team and company level depend on group dynamics, such as communications and coordinated efforts. Participants who describe both sides of knowledge transfers can offer more complete perspectives than those who relate to just one side.

Stories. Clinical questions about learning lead to abstract answers, but stories and anecdotes can help people vividly recall their learning practices. Ask interviewees to remember incidents when change took place rapidly and effectively, when they mastered new processes, or when a good practice was diffused rapidly throughout the organization.

Artifacts. Anthropologists search for artifacts that offer tangible clues of how a society behaved. What artifacts might a learning assessment find? For example, publicly displayed performance scorecards, often seen in production facilities, show a concern for measurement and feedback.

Ongoing Assessment

The assessment process can provide a wonderful opportunity to train staff members in learning principles. Scientists from Hawthorne to Heisenberg have discovered that measuring a process inevitably causes it to be altered. In the same way, when learning is measured, learning processes are altered. With this in mind, you can design assessment interviews to serve as training in the principles of organizational learning, and improve your learning state even as you measure it.

Above all, it is important to continue to measure your company's learning activities over time. Conducting an initial learning assessment can provide a valuable baseline of learning practices against which to evaluate progress, but overall assessment should become an ongoing part of the organizational learning process. This is especially important because the learning needs of a company will change as it revises its vision and strategy. Making progress on the journey toward creating a learning organization requires a continual realignment between the goals of the company and its chosen learning path. ⌒

Reprinted with permission from Arthur D. Little, from the Third Quarter 1995 issue of *Prism*, Arthur D. Little's journal for senior managers.

Nils Bohlin is a vice president of Arthur D. Little International and coordinator of its global Pharmaceutical Industry Practice, based in Stockholm. He is also the leader of Arthur D. Little's learning organization project in Europe.

Paul Brenner is president of Arthur D. Little Program Systems Management Company, specializing in information and program management services to government and industry.

About the Authors

Nils Bohlin is a vice president of Arthur D. Little International and coordinator of its global Pharmaceutical Industry Practice, based in Stockholm. He is also the leader of Arthur D. Little's learning organization project in Europe.

Paul Brenner is president of Arthur D. Little Program Systems Management Company, specializing in information and program management services to government and industry.

Tim Gallwey is credited with founding the field of sports psychology. His four bestselling books on The Inner Game have deeply influenced the worlds of business and sports. For the last 15 years, Tim has spent most of his time working with companies that want to find a better way to implement change.

Arie de Geus was appointed executive vice president at the Royal Dutch/Shell Group in 1978 and was with the company for 38 years. He served as head of an advisory group to the World Bank from 1990 to 1993, and is a visiting fellow at London Business School. He is the author of the well-regarded *The Living Company* (Harvard Business School Press, 1997).

Kazimierz Gozdz is a partner in the Corporate Civility Group and a consulting member of the Society for Organizational Learning. Kaz has worked to build theory, practice, and methods for transforming organiza-

113

tions into thriving learning communities. He writes, speaks, and consults in the area of workplace community, serving as editor for *Community Building: Renewing Spirit and Learning in Business* (New Leaders Press, 1995) and as coauthor, with Peter M. Senge and Joseph Jaworski, of *Setting the Field: Creating the Conditions for Profound Institutional Change* (Society for Organizational Learning working paper).

Daniel H. Kim, PhD, is publisher of *The Systems Thinker* and a trustee on the governing council of the Society for Organizational Learning (SoL). He is a well-regarded author as well as an international public speaker, facilitator, and teacher of systems thinking and organizational learning.

Art Kleiner is coauthor and editorial director of *The Fifth Discipline Fieldbook* (Doubleday, 1994) and author of *The Age of Heretics* (Doubleday, 1996), a history of the social movement to change large corporations for the better.

Bill O'Brien was the chief executive officer of Hanover Insurance Company until his retirement in 1991. During his 21-year tenure at Hanover, Bill coauthored a business philosophy that resulted in a significant corporate turnaround. By applying the concepts of organizational learning, he and his staff created one of the most respected companies in the insurance industry, both in terms of the work environment and its profitability.

Edgar H. Schein is Sloan Fellows professor of management emeritus and a senior lecturer at the Sloan School of Management. He is the author of numerous books on organization development.

Peter M. Senge is a senior lecturer at the Massachusetts Institute of Technology, where he is part of the Organizational Learning and Change group. He is also chairman of the Society for Organizational Learning. He is the author of the widely acclaimed book *The Fifth Discipline: The*

Art and Practice of the Learning Organization, and, with colleagues Charlotte Roberts, Rick Ross, Bryan Smith, and Art Kleiner, coauthor of *The Fifth Discipline Fieldbook: Strategies and Tools for Building a Learning Organization*.

Bryan Smith is coauthor of *The Fifth Discipline Fieldbook* and president of Innovation Associates of Canada (Toronto, Ontario).

Greg Zlevor is president of Westwood International, a consulting company specializing in organizational and teamwork strategies for business and groups. He is also the founder of the *Community in Organizations Conference*, an annual event that investigates creative relationships within organizations.

About the Artist

Nancy Margulies creates visual records of events using a process she developed called Mindscaping. She regularly contributes to Pegasus Communications' *Systems Thinking in Action*™ Conference, and her illustrations have appeared frequently in *The Systems Thinker*™ Newsletter. She is a consultant to business and community groups and lives in St. Louis, Missouri. Her illustrations appear on pp. 14, 22, 34, 36, and 44 of this book.

Additional Resources

De Geus, Arie, *The Living Company* (Harvard Business School Press, 1997)

Gallwey, Tim, *The Inner Game of Work* (Random House, 1998)

Gozdz, Kazimierz (ed.), *Community Building: Renewing Spirit and Learning in Business* (Sterling and Stone, 1995)

Jaworski, Joseph, *Synchronicity: The Inner Path of Leadership* (Berrett-Koehler, 1996)

Kim, Daniel H., *Toward Learning Organizations: Integrating Total Quality Control and Systems Thinking* (Pegasus Communications, 1997)

Kleiner, Art, *The Age of Heretics* (Doubleday, 1996)

Leverage: News and Ideas for the Organizational Learner (newsletter) (Pegasus Communications)

O'Brien, Bill, *The Soul of Corporate Leadership: Guidelines for Values-Centered Governance* (Pegasus Communications, 1998)

Peck, M. Scott, *The Different Drum: Community Making and Peace* (Simon & Schuster, Inc., 1987)

Schein, Edgar H., *Organizational Culture and Leadership* (Jossey-Bass, 1992)

Senge, Peter, *The Fifth Discipline: The Art and Practice of the Learning Organization* (Doubleday, 1990)

Senge, Peter; Art Kleiner, Charlotte Roberts, Richard Ross, Bryan Smith, *The Fifth Discipline Fieldbook* (Doubleday, 1994)

The Systems Thinker (newsletter) (Pegasus Communications)

Wardman, Kellie T. (ed.), *Reflections on Creating Learning Organizations* (Pegasus Communications, 1994)

Wardman O'Reilly, Kellie (ed.), *Managing the Rapids: Stories from the Forefront of the Learning Organization* (Pegasus Communications, 1995)

Wheatley, Margaret, *Leadership and the New Science* (Berrett-Koehler, 1993)

Index
to The Systems Thinker™

From Fragmentation to Integration: Building Learning Communities
Peter M. Senge and Daniel H. Kim (V8N4, May 1997)

Is There More to Corporations Than Maximizing Profits?
Bryan Smith and Art Kleiner (V6N3, April 1995)

The "Living" Company: Extending the Corporate Lifeline
Arie de Geus (V7N4, May 1996)

Transforming the Character of a Corporation
Bill O'Brien (V7N2, March 1996)

Rethinking Leadership in the Learning Organization
Peter M. Senge (V7N1, February 1996)

Can Learning Cultures Evolve?
Edgar H. Schein (V7N6, August 1996)

The Inner Game of Work: Building Capability in the Workplace
Tim Gallwey (V8N6, August 1997)

Creating a New Workplace: Making a Commitment to Community
Greg Zlevor (V5N7, September 1994)

Building a Core Competence in Community
Kazimierz Gozdz (V6N2, March 1995)

The Learning Organization Journey: Assessing and Valuing Progress
Nils Bohlin and Paul Brenner (V7N5, June/July 1996)